W9-APO-372

GREAT LADY OF THE THEATRE

Sarah Bernhardt

Born: October 22, 1844
Died: March 26, 1923

Books by Iris Noble

NELLIE BLY: First Woman Reporter
JOSEPH PULITZER: Front Page Pioneer
CLARENCE DARROW: Defense Attorney
THE DOCTOR WHO DARED: William Osler
ONE GOLDEN SUMMER
GREAT LADY OF THE THEATRE: Sarah Bernhardt

GREAT LADY
of the THEATRE
Sarah Bernhardt

BY

IRIS NOBLE

Julian Messner, Inc.   •   *New York*

subj. ok.

Published by Julian Messner, Inc.
8 West 40 Street, New York 18

Published simultaneously in Canada
by The Copp Clark Publishing Co. Limited

Jacket photograph used by courtesy of Culver Service

Printed in the United States of America

Library of Congress Catalog Card No. 60–7052

To Sally,
with affection
and gratitude

AUTHOR'S NOTE

The search for the story of Sarah Bernhardt started in America before I left for Europe in January of 1959. It was possible to find people who had seen her act on the American stage, newspaper men who had interviewed her, and there was even one acquaintance who had acted in a minor role in her company while she was on tour of the western states. Here, too, I began the reading of the plays she had made famous, reading them in French so that they would not suffer from translations.

In Rome I found in a bookstore an old, tattered book with title and front pages torn off. Among its chapters on the theatre was one written by Sarah Bernhardt—her instructions for acting, called "The Art of the Theatre," an article which has been long out of print and unavailable.

Naturally, the real research was done in Paris. Here I was fortunate in meeting and talking with both the assistant-director of the Conservatoire and the Secretary-General of the Comédie Française. They were most kind and helpful, giving me many hours of their time and supplying me with the rich background of both institutions as well as numerous stories of Mademoiselle Bernhardt. Also in Paris I visited her own theatre, the Théâtre Sarah Bernhardt.

The Bibliotheque L'Arsenal in Paris was a treasure-house library of theatrical books and manuscripts, old pictures and theatrical playbills. Sarah Bernhardt's own memoirs, MY DOUBLE LIFE, out of print now, were there. These memoirs were unfinished and only told of her early life, but they gave me insight into her personality and character. In the Bibliotheque, too, were bound collections of the reviews of the famous critic, Francisque Sarcey; the ENCYCLO-PEDIE DU THÉÂTRE CONTEMPORAIN by Gilles Guant and Frederick Towarnicki, published by Les Publications de France, with magnificent portraits of Sarah Bernhardt and fine word-pictures of her acting in her most noted roles; the DICTIONNAIRE DES BIOGRAPHIES, published by Presses Universitaires de France, 1958, under the direction of Pierre Grimal.

Of earlier biographies of Sarah Bernhardt, two were particularly informative: Maurice Baring's SARAH BERNHARDT, published by the University Press, Edinburgh in 1933, and Louis Verneuil's THE FABULOUS LIFE OF SARAH BERNHARDT, Harper and Bros., Publishers, New York, 1942. As background studies of the theatre I wish to acknowledge the help I received from: Mordecai Gorelik's NEW THEATRES FOR OLD, Vail-Ballou Press of Binghamton, New York, 1955; Llody Morris' CURTAIN TIME, Random House, New York, 1953; Henry James' THE SCENIC ART, Rutgers University Press, New Brunswick, 1948.

Iris Noble

[1]

There would come a time when she would be famous and rich, worshiped and adored, when she would be clothed in furs and jewels and a red carpet would be unrolled for her to walk upon.

But that was in the future.

This, now, was 1848 and she was four years old and her tiny feet were wet and muddy through the little patched shoes that splashed in the cobblestones; her ragged, dirty dress did nothing to keep out the cold. She was miserable, half crying. Titine, her new friend, tried to console her as the two crouched shivering over the Paris street gutter.

"Don't cry, Sarah," Titine said. "See? If you put this stick here in the water, it will go all the way down the stones to the middle of the street—just like it was a boat floating down the Seine River." Titine was a city urchin. Her only toys had been just such sticks and stones floating on rain puddles. "And if we put a bit of colored paper on it, we can play it's a flower."

Sarah was not comforted. Sticks were not boats. Dirty rainwater was not a river. "I don't want to play. There was a real pond on the farm—all clean—and I had a real boat with a real sail on it. And there were real flowers and I could pick them, all I wanted. My nurse calls me 'gillyflower' 'cause that's the flower I like best."

Titine drew in her breath sharply. She didn't want to think that Sarah was telling lies, but who ever heard of being able to pick all the flowers you wanted? Flowers grew in parks, just to look at, or were sold by flower girls to rich ladies. They weren't for poor children. "What's a nurse?" she asked to change the subject.

Sarah pointed a thin, grubby finger up at the window overhead where a woman was peering out, watching the two small girls.

"Her," Sarah said. "She's my nurse. My Mama said she was to take care of me. First we were at the farm and then we were at another place. And Mama and my Auntie Rosine used to come and see me and bring me beautiful presents and little cakes to eat and new shoes and dolls. Mama is pretty and smells so nice. But she doesn't come any more. Nurse says Mama doesn't know where I am. I don't want to be here." Her eyes filled with tears again. "I want to go back to the farm! I want Mama to come!" And with a sudden outburst of childish rage at all the strange and awful things that had so suddenly happened to her small world, Sarah Bernhardt threw a stone that hit the stick-boat and knocked it out of the puddle.

"Aw, look what you done!" Titine jumped to her feet. She was bigger. She wanted to slap Sarah. But she had learned in a very short time that her friend's tempers were fearsome things and that when Sarah was angry she was not afraid of anyone, no matter what size. So Titine just yelled, "You're a bad girl!" and ran off to find someone else to play with.

Left alone, Sarah felt a little better after her outburst. She had wanted to hit something and she had; now the temper had dried up her tears for the moment.

She sat back on a stone that was drier than the rest, wrapped her arms around her skinny body, and moodily watched the street and the people on it. Two women with shawls on their heads and baskets on their arms gossiped in high, clackety voices as they walked slowly by on the opposite side; a boy went by carrying long loaves of bread, like sticks, in one hand. An old man plodded slowly along, shivering in the chill day in spite of his heavy cloak. A cart pulled by a tired gray horse stopped down the street and a shop-keeper in his leather apron came out to unload wood from the cart —fine wood from which he made the pretty tables that she could see in his shop windows.

"Sarah, are you warm enough, child? Don't you want to come inside?" her nurse called from the upper window. Her voice was kind and tender and the child smiled in spite of her misery. She

10

liked the nurse very much, but the nurse liked that man she called her "husband" more than she did Sarah. It was better to stay down here than to go up to that crowded room. That husband might be there.

"I want to stay here, please," she called back.

The woman's head disappeared from the window. Sarah brooded over that man who had married her nurse and brought them to this place. He wasn't a bad man, but why had he done this? Why had her nurse wanted to come here with him, when she and Sarah had been so happy out in the country? Here, her nurse had to work so hard cleaning for other people. Here, the three of them had to sleep and eat and live in that one, horrible, dark old room.

The ways of grownups were too strange for her to understand and she turned her attention back to the street.

She jumped to her feet. A very handsome dark green and silver-painted carriage had turned the corner and was rolling down the cobblestones toward her. She opened her eyes wide at the beautiful brown horse and the coachman sitting up in front in his dark green uniform, with the reins in one hand and a little whip in the other. The carriage was stopping—right next door! It was such an unusual event that even the gossiping housewives stopped to look and the shopkeeper held a block of wood poised on his arm while he stared. Sarah hopped first on one foot and then on the other so that she could get a better look at the carriage.

The coachman-driver climbed down and opened the door.

First there was a tiny foot in a black silk slipper on the carriage step, then the rustle and swirl of gray silk skirts with a froth of white lace petticoats just showing as the lady stepped down, holding on to the driver's arm for balance. A gray silk bonnet hid the lady's face, but Sarah could see the lovely red and black ribbons on it and the red buttons down the front of the tiny waist.

The lady glanced at the shop in front of her. It was a glove-maker's. She looked down at a scrap of paper in her hand, then nodded her head and turned to give her coachman some instructions. As she did so, she turned so that Sarah could look her full in the face.

The little girl's heart gave a great bound in her chest. For a

11

second she couldn't move. She couldn't believe it. Then she screamed, "Aunt Rosine! Aunt Rosine!"

The lady, who had been about to enter the shop, stopped short and looked back, startled.

"Auntie Rosine—it's me. It's Sarah!" she was running on her thin little legs, stumbling a bit over the stones. She could hardly breathe. Her screams were jerked out of her throat. She flung herself onto the lady's skirts. "Auntie Rosine, you did come, you did!"

Rosine Van Hard was more than startled. Who was this filthy child to be calling her "aunt"? Surely not Sarah, not Julie's child —yet who else could it be? She stared into the upturned face and tried to pull away from the clinging fingers; then suddenly, through the dirt on that face and the dreadful clothes on that small body, she saw that it was really and certainly Sarah.

"Child! Child, what are you doing here in Paris? Look at you. Where is that nurse of yours? My poor infant, I don't understand any of this. I just don't understand. What will your mother say?" She happened to look up and saw the nurse's excited face in the window. "So there she is. Well, I'll have a word with her about this. Come Sarah. Don't pull my frock like that, child. Your hands are dirty and this is a new gown and I am lunching with the Countess in less than half an hour."

They walked up the stairs together, Sarah laughing and crying with joy, her Aunt Rosine fluttering ahead with a volley of "I don't understand" and "I can't make this out" and "La, la—what an extraordinary affair!" A peculiar business, indeed this was, for an aunt to find the niece she supposed safely tucked away on a farm wearing pretty starched dresses and drinking good milk, growing fat on eggs and butter, here in Paris and looking like a dirty street gamin.

The nurse was waiting for them with the door opened at the second-floor landing. She started to speak almost before she could see them.

". . . so it wasn't my fault at all, Miss Rosine. I hadn't a word from her mother for such a long time and no money from her and when I came to her address in Paris they told me she had gone

12

to Poland for a visit and nobody knew when she would be back——"

Rosine waved a gloved hand to check the flow of words. "I remember that Julie moved you from the farm in Brittany to Neuilly, so you would be closer to Paris. But I can't understand why you are living here or why my niece looks like a ragged scarecrow." Her pretty face was petulant. She looked about the one crowded room with a shudder.

"Well, it's like this, Miss. Her mother forgot to send me any money, so I couldn't buy her clothes or pay the rent at Neuilly. Then I was being courted and I wanted to get married and I was at my wits' end to know what to do. My man had this job, taking care of the rooms and apartments in this building, and he was willing for me to bring Sarah along with me. It's not much of a job, but it would do fine for the two of us. We're young. But its hard on the child and there's no money for anything but her food. She has to sleep behind that curtain there."

Rosine looked about her with a sigh. She was no longer angry with the nurse. It was just like her sister to go flying off with never a thought that the nurse and child wouldn't be just where she put them. Such a miserable room this was! One room for living and sleeping and eating. Still, the nurse had a good heart and liked the child, that was something.

"That's just like my sister Julie," she said, forgetting that she had almost gone with her to Poland and had only just returned from a madcap pleasure trip to Naples. "Running off and forgetting to make arrangements before she left."

"I'm so thankful you came along. I've been so worried that her mother wouldn't know where she was or where to find her," the nurse said, looking over to where Sarah was busy behind her curtain.

"Yes, I suppose so." Rosine's pretty, flighty face was clouded. She was kind, but she was also young and as thoughtless and self-centered as her sister. It was one thing to be indignant at Sarah in rags; it was another thing to find the nurse looking to her, expecting her to be responsible. And she had to meet the Countess in just fifteen minutes.

13

Then her face brightened. She reached for her purse. "But now there is nothing to worry about, is there? I can tell Julie where Sarah is when she returns—which should be soon. In the meantime she is better off with you: you can rent the room next door for her and buy her some new clothes. Here is my address. When this money is gone, you can come to me for more. Keep some of these francs for your trouble. Yes, it's all so unfortunate, but really not so serious. Sarah likes you. Buy her some trinkets and toys and, please do wash her face. She was never a pretty baby and now . . ." Aunt Rosine rolled her big blue eyes in dismay.

She got up, putting her finger to her lips and nodding in Sarah's direction. The child's back was turned. A look passed between Rosine and the nurse. They understood each other. It would be better for Rosine to slip away without the child's noticing that she was gone.

Sarah, busily packing her few little possessions into a box, didn't listen to any of this adult conversation. It never entered her head that she wouldn't be leaving this awful place with her aunt. When she turned suddenly and caught her aunt going out the door, when Aunt Rosine had to stop and bend down and kiss her quickly and tell her to be a good girl and mind her nurse and say something more about lunching with a Countess, Sarah didn't know what to make of it. Not until the door closed upon the swish of silken skirts, not until she heard the sound of those little slippers running down the steps, did she understand.

She flew to the open window.

"Aunt Rosine . . .?" Her voice was shrill with panic.

Below, her aunt hurried out of the doorway and her voice floated sweetly up: "I must go, darling. I'm late now. You mustn't worry. Your Mama will be back soon. See, I'll blow you a kiss."

Sarah stared, unbelieving. Her aunt was going. She was walking over to the carriage. She was giving her arm to the coachman.

"Now don't make a fuss, little one. Let's have none of your tantrums, Sarah." The nurse's voice came from behind her, kindly but firm, and there was a rustle of banknotes as she counted the money Rosine had left.

14

Sarah's whole being was centered on what was happening on the street below. A passion of longing, a terrible feeling of desolation, was shaking her body. Her aunt was disappearing into the carriage. The coachman was closing the door. It was going to happen. Aunt Rosine was going to ride off and leave her there. The coachman was climbing up onto his high perch, and when he took the reins in his hands and lifted the whip, the carriage wheels would roll and the horse would move and Aunt Rosine would be gone and she would be left behind to be cold and dirty and to cry in the night.

"No! No!"

Sarah didn't know she was screaming this. She didn't hear the gasp of her nurse behind her. She didn't know she had climbed so that she stood in the open window, her feet on the sill. There was one second when she knew that it was a terrible, scary long way down, then she shut her eyes and jumped.

At the nurse's scream, Rosine stuck her head out of the carriage window just in time to see the tiny body hurtling down. She was almost out of the carriage when she heard the sickening sound on the tiny body hitting the sharp, jagged stones of the streets. Her heart almost stopped with shock. It was the coachman, tumbling pell-mell off his perch, who picked Sarah up; it was the shopkeeper across the street who ran over and wiped some of the blood off on his leather apron.

But still the blood streamed from the child's knee and from her arm, soaking the front of her dress; one arm, Rosine saw, dangled at a peculiar angle from Sarah's shoulder.

Sarah knew nothing of all this. She was hardly conscious. Voices seemed to come from far, far away, as if she were dreaming. There was a terrible pain, but the only thing that mattered was that she knew she was being lifted up and into Aunt Rosine's carriage. She was on Aunt Rosine's lap. The pretty face was bending over her and the soft voice was crooning, "Oh, you poor baby, poor baby," then she fainted and knew nothing more.

When Sarah woke up she was in a strange bed and a strange man was doing things to her arm that hurt so much she went to sleep again. Then there were a few days with nothing but pain and she was fiery hot and thirsty. The doctor came again and again to put those white wrappings around her knee and shoulder. There was one evening of glorious happiness when she smelled the perfume and heard the voice that could only be Mama's.

"Do you mean to tell me my Sarah jumped over ten feet to the ground? Onto those stones? Why, she might have been killed."

It didn't matter that Mama's voice sounded as cross as it sounded horrified. The pain and the fuzzy sleep began again, but she knew that she was in Aunt Rosine's house and Mama was there too. That was all that mattered.

Even when, as the days went on and the pain was less and her head was clear enough so that she could understand what was being said and she knew that Mama was angry at her for what she had done, she was still glad to be here instead of with the nurse. The nurse was kind and Mama was not; it didn't make any difference, though it hurt in a way that was worse than the pain in her shoulder.

Julie's light, treble voice, which usually tinkled with laughter, was angry and shocked as she talked over Sarah's bed to Rosine. Her large, round blue eyes were hard; her mouth pouted. "I never heard of a child doing such a thing. She always was such a determined, obstinate, self-willed little thing, always screaming to have her own way. She upset my nerves so much, it was really better for her to be with the nurse. Now what am I going to do? The doctor says she will recover, but I can't send her to another nurse. There's no knowing what she might do next. Oh, dear—and I had such a charming apartment selected. It just suits me and now I will have to turn my boudoir-sitting room into a room for Sarah and there will be doctors and nurses and that horrid smell of medicine everywhere."

Aunt Rosine's voice was sympathetic. "I know—it is difficult. So strange she should be your child, when she doesn't take after you at all. I should have expected you to have a sweet, pretty, obedient little girl. But, after all, it won't be for long. In less than a year you can begin thinking of schools for her."

"A year!" Mama cried.

Sarah thought the room in her mother's apartment, where she was moved shortly, was the most beautiful she had ever seen. It was like heaven to be in it and be clean and have servants to wash her and dress her. The dislocated shoulder healed quickly, but the broken kneecap kept her in bed for months. She didn't mind. Child though she was, she knew it was better for her to lie there quietly, where she could listen for the sound of Mama's laugh and see her once in a while dressed up in her lovely clothes, coming in to kiss her lightly on her way to the other rooms where there were always people and excitement.

If Sarah had been up and about, she would have had to go into those other rooms and meet the people and she knew that Mama would not have liked that. Dimly the child knew she was something called "ugly" and that grown-up ladies and gentlemen did not like ugly children.

Sometimes the maids forgot and left Sarah's door open a little in the evening. Then she could hear people laughing or listening to music or talking. The deep, deep voices were the men; the light, gay ones were the ladies.

"Tell us how you liked Poland, Julie."

"Oh my dears, it was just delightful at first. There were balls every evening in those marvelous old castles. But then the weather changed and it was terrible. You have no idea how simply grim those castles can be without any heat. I began to long for my beautiful Paris, so I simply ran away without telling anyone and came home."

In the darkness Sarah lay, imagining the soft pout to her mother's lips and the dancing lights in her eyes. A gentleman was probably bending over her hand. Sarah could hear the smooth, masculine drawl:

"Really, Julie, you are much too beautiful and charming to waste on Poland."

Then one of the maids would discover the partly opened door and close it firmly. "There now, it's time for you to be going to sleep. I'll brush your hair for you if you like. Such thick, curly hair! Pity it snarls so easily. And it's a funny color—not like your mother's smooth yellow hair at all, though yours looks nice too, when it's brushed like this. There. Move over while I straighten this sheet. The doctor says the bandages will be coming off quite soon."

It was almost a year before Sarah was well enough to walk and run like other children. Almost immediately she was whisked off to a boarding school. It happened so fast that she hardly had time to realize she was once again being sent away from her mother until several weeks had passed. The school was a poor one, with teachers who were indifferent about everything. Sarah hated it and began to long once more for her mother with an intensity that would have amazed that thoughtless woman.

One day her father arrived at school. Sarah had seen him only twice before. He always came so abruptly and left so quickly that she had a hard time remembering what he looked like, except that he was handsome.

He was as irresponsible as her mother; lazy, wealthy, and of a very good French family. Since he was fond of nothing but traveling and his own pleasure, he saw little of Julie or Sarah, but he did provide well for them. He had even included in his will the sum of one hundred thousand francs to be given to Sarah when she married.

Now he had one of his infrequent attacks of conscience and had come to see about his daughter's welfare. Almost at a glance he saw that the school was third-rate, teaching the little girl nothing, not even paying any attention to her social graces or her spiritual life. He insisted that she be sent at once to the Catholic Convent of Grandchamps at Versailles, where he knew the scholastic training was of an unusually high standard. Julie agreed; it mattered very little to her. Sarah's father, who was just a tall stranger to her, took her to Mother Sainte-Sophie at the convent.

After one look at Mother Sainte-Sophie's round face beaming out of the black veil, the sweetness and tenderness of her smile, the round, comfortable plumpness of her person, Sarah loved her immediately. She let go her father's hand and reached out to the nun's. Mother Sainte-Sophie drew her into her arms instead.

"We will take good care of your little girl, Monsieur," she said in her sweet, sensible voice. "I'm sure she is both good and intelligent; we will do our best to teach her and make her happy." She squeezed Sarah gently to let her know there was nothing to worry about in this strange place.

Sarah's father left, satisfied the girl was in good hands. It was the last time she saw him, for he died a few years later. What memory she had of him was to fade quickly, so that she could hardly remember whether he was fair and dark, only that he was tall and that it was difficult for him to know how to talk to a child.

❧{ 2 }❧

Sarah remained at the convent for eight years. Her love for Mother Sainte-Sophie grew and deepened. Because she was treated with kindness and understanding, she threw herself into her studies with a vigor that astonished everyone. She tried hard to be obedient and please the nuns.

It wasn't always a successful try. As much as she wanted to, she could not always be obedient. Life for Sarah was lived with such intensity that she couldn't help but get into trouble.

"I don't know what comes over the child at times," Sister Seraphine confided to Mother Sainte-Sophie. "She can be so good, she will work so hard for days and show extraordinary brilliance in her classes. Then some little thing will happen and she flies into a temper. Yesterday she was very rude. She pulled another girl's hair just because the other girl asked her if she had a nice vacation at home during the Christmas holidays."

Mother Sainte-Sophie's smile was tinged with pity. "I rather think Sarah did not have a nice vacation at home. The poor girl has suffered a great deal of slighting and lack of affection from

19

those who should be closest to her. Another child might respond to such treatment by becoming sullen or afraid of life; Sarah's reaction is to fight back. She doesn't know yet that she can't make up for the hurt she receives from her mother by pulling someone's hair for it."

The two nuns paced the flower-bordered courtyard. Over in one corner, prominent because of her unruly mop of tawny gold hair, was the subject of their conversation in the center of a circle of other girls.

"You always see her like that, in the center of things," commented Sister Seraphine. "She is always the leader, whether it is in doing good schoolwork or in climbing the school walls because she *must* see what is on the other side."

"I know. She has a remarkable spark of vitality in her. When she channels it into hard work I am amazed at what she can do." Mother Sainte-Sophie worried at times over her indulgent weakness for this one girl among so many. "Such energy! Sometimes I think any misbehavior of hers is just the need for that energy to spill over; it can't be held back by our rules and discipline."

Sarah was baptized "Sarah Rosine Marie Henriette Bernhardt." All too soon her school days came to an end. Just before her graduation the school put on a little religious play and Sarah took the part of the Angel Gabriel. She was neither better nor worse than the other girls, but Mother Sainte-Sophie was at least able to compliment her on her voice.

"You spoke very clearly and distinctly, Sarah."

Good-byes were said with a great many tears on Sarah's part and a good deal of affectionate counsel—and a good deal of inward anxiety—on the part of Mother Sainte-Sophie.

The abrupt change from the discipline, the busy, quiet, orderly life of the convent to the hectic frivolity of her mother's house was a shock to Sarah. There was luxury and money to spend in Paris; she no longer had to wear the plain uniforms of the school. She had had more schooling than most girls of her time. She was considered old enough to become a part of the bigger world.

But she was completely lost in it. She hated her mother's life and the constant round of parties and balls, musicales and theaters, the gossip about clothes and fashion that started so early in the morning when smart carriages would pull up outside her mother's apartment in the rue St.-Honoré and smartly dressed ladies would come in to chatter over the breakfast chocolate with her mother; this life which would end each day with gentlemen calling, bringing with them the latest scandal, the latest jokes, the latest tidbit of political news.

"I hate it," Sarah confided to her only friend, quiet little Madame Guerard who lived in a modest apartment upstairs. Sarah's face was twisted in a grimace; her eyes were fiery. "I hate all that silly gossip. How can they spend so many hours talking about whether pleated skirts are coming into style or whether hats will have feathers or ribbons on them? I wish I could be like them because it would please Mama, but I can't. Look at me! I'm all bones and I'm too tall and I can't mince and glide about the way they do when they walk."

Madame Guerard looked at the dress Sarah was wearing and sighed. Privately she thought that the simple convent uniform had suited the girl better than all these ruffles and bows and puffed sleeves. The dress hung on Sarah's thin body like a sack.

"Couldn't you try just a little harder, Sarah dear? It means so much to your mother to have smiling faces around her. It does make her cross when you are rude to her guests." Madame Guerard was a widow and childless; and for some reason she couldn't explain she was drawn to this strange girl.

"I do try. But I'm not pretty and I'm not graceful and I don't know what to say when some awful man kisses my hand and says, 'How charming you are, Mademoiselle.'" She mimicked the expression of a bored but gallant elderly man. "He knows and I know that I'm not charming at all and it's a lie."

"You can be charming when you want to, Sarah. When you are with me you can laugh and be gay. Your whole face changes then.

Sarah cradled her elbows in her hands and rocked back and forth on Madame Guerard's faded brown hassock. She brooded. "I did try, the other evening. I brushed my hair so hard I made all the curls lay down smooth and I wore that new green silk gown and remembered to smile all the time; I lowered my eyes when the ladies said I looked nice and I agreed with everyone no matter what they said. There was one man there, about fifty years old, and he paid a lot of attention to me—Mama was so pleased. I even remembered to duck my head down and giggle, the way I've seen other girls do, when he paid me a lot of silly compliments. And do you know what happened?" Sarah raised shocked eyes to Madame Guerard's. "He wants to marry me!"

"What!"

"Oh yes. Mama thinks it is wonderful. He has money and when I marry I'll get my hundred thousand francs. She says I should do it."

Madame Guerard's heart contracted. She was furiously angry at Sarah's mother. This must not happen—to marry the girl off to a man so much older—just because Julie wanted to get rid of her and because there would be money.

"What do you want to do, if not get married?" she forced herself to ask in a calm way.

"I want to be a nun!" Sarah said passionately. It seemed to her that the convent was a haven of peace. She yearned for that quiet, purposeful life.

She said it again, the very next night, to her mother. "I want to be a nun." This time she said it frantically and yet earnestly.

Julie had called together a few of her best friends to help her decide what was to be done with this daughter of hers, especially since she was turning down this very good offer of marriage. Julie was quite put out about Sarah's refusal. A nun indeed. Anyone could see that the girl, with her sudden, tempestuous, stormy nature, was not cut out for the religious life.

But if not a nun and if she wouldn't marry, then what?

Sarah had been placed in a chair, in one corner of the charming little drawing room, and the others had ringed themselves around her as if she were an object to study and discuss.

"It is a pity," the Duc de Morny said, looking at Sarah over the rim of his champagne glass, "that she doesn't resemble you, Julie. She has your long eyelashes—those unusually long ones—but with her eyes they just look odd. Such strange eyes. Like a cat's. In fact, with her face so thin and with such a pointed chin, she does resemble a Siamese cat. Now if she were pretty, she might expect an offer of marriage from a younger man who might please her." He looked at Sarah's half-closed eyes again and was startled when they suddenly opened to blaze a fierce, silent rebellion at him. "No, no," he said hastily, "we shall have to think of something besides marriage."

"But what?" Julie was annoyed. She liked life to be amusing. This child and her problems were anything but amusing.

"Why not let her enter the convent?" another gentleman suggested.

Mademoiselle Brabender, a close friend of her mother's, objected. "Utterly unsuitable," she said, reaching over to select a bonbon from a crystal dish on the table. "She is not the type."

The Duc de Morny burst out laughing. "Observe the girl! Look at her—she is trying to show us what a good nun she would be."

In fact that is just what Sarah was doing. She wanted to go back to the convent so desperately, away from people who made fun of her and called her a cat, that she was determined to show them she was the type. She had arranged her hands in a pious manner, a meekness had come over her face and her shoulders. Consciously she had willed into her mind the face of Sister Seraphine and her own had become amazingly like it, with the same expression of sweet patience and gentle serenity.

"Don't be absurd, Sarah," her mother said sharply.

The Duc was struck by an idea. "Perhaps that is your answer. If she can mimic, probably she could be taught to act. Why not send her to the Conservatoire?"

Julie frowned. "She's much too thin." But it was an idea and not too preposterous. The Conservatoire was the famous school of dramatic art where young girls and boys were trained for the French stage. After all, if Sarah would not marry, what other career was open to her? "But would she be accepted? I believe hundreds of young people strive every year to enter the Conservatoire, which accepts only thirty-five of the best. It is even difficult to get an audition."

The Duc shrugged. "With my influence I can at least assure her of an audition, an examination. Beyond that, I don't know." He rose. "It will be up to her."

The discussion had somehow come to an end; the Duc had made up their minds. Mademoiselle Brabender offered to improve Sarah's diction before the audition would take place. Sarah was dismissed to go to her room.

She went, puzzled by her strange, mixed-up feelings. Though she wasn't aware of it then, her desire to become a nun was not prompted so much by deep religious conviction as it was by the desire to escape to the one place where she had been happy. The Conservatoire, she thought. I don't want to go. Yet, in spite of herself, she was excited by the thought that *something* was going to happen.

The next day Mademoiselle Brabender gave her exercises to do: "Every morning, in your room, I want you to sing 'do, re, mi, fa, sol' up the scale. After lunch, you are to say forty times: '*Un très gros rat dans un très gros trou,*' to open your 'r.' After dinner forty times say this: '*Combien ces six saucisses-ci? C'est six sous, ces six saucissons-ci*'—in order to stop you from hissing the 's.' At night in bed say twenty times: '*Didon, dina, dit-on, du, dos, d'un, dodu, dindon*' and twenty times: '*Le plus petit papa, petit popo, petit papa*'—to open your mouth wide for the 'd' and to help form the 'p.'"

Sarah giggled. She ran up the stairs to tell Madame Guerard and could hardly speak for laughing. "Oh, listen to me! '*Un très gros rat dans un très gros trou*'—'A very large rat in a very large hole!'" she said, pronouncing the 'r' with an exaggerated roll to it. "And I have to say forty times a day: '*Combien ces six saucisses-ci? C'est six sous, ces six saucisses-ci*'—'How much are these six sausages? They are six sous, these sausages!'" she fell on Madame Guerard's sofa, flat on her stomach, laughing, kicking her heels up in the air.

Madame was delighted with the change in her young friend. When Sarah was happy like this, everything was different about her. She seemed to lose her coltish awkwardness. Her eyes, which seemed half-closed in that long, upward, slanting slit when she

24

was sullen, were wide open and radiant. There were dancing lights in them.

You even notice, thought Madame with surprise, how fine and pearly is her skin.

"But you will practice surely?" she asked.

Sarah tossed her head and wiped her eyes. She had laughed so much she cried. "Of, of course. It's all foolishness. I don't want to be an actress, but it is something to *do*. I am so tired of doing nothing."

"Then I will lend you some of my books," Madame Guerard told her. "Here"—going to the bookcase—"is Racine. He is one of France's greatest writers of plays. And here is Molière and Corneille, two more great ones. Take them and read them, then come and read them aloud to me." If having something to do and keeping busy would make Sarah happy, the older woman would see to it she was well occupied.

In the remaining weeks before the yearly examination at the Conservatoire, Sarah faithfully practiced her exercises. She liked the plays but she preferred poetry; she enjoyed the sound of it when she read it out loud. Fontaine's *Fables* were her favorites.

All this was something her active mind enjoyed. It satisfied a love of beauty in her, a drive in her for hard work and—just as important—it kept her out of her mother's drawing room and away from parties.

When the day of Sarah's tryout arrived, Julie had forgotten all about it. She had another engagement for the day. "I *am* sorry, Sarah, but you see how it is. I can't go with you." She was dressed in her long black riding habit, ready for a canter in the park. She wasn't going to change her plans, regardless of the pleading and consternation in Sarah's face. "I know! Run up and ask Madame Guerard if she won't go. She's a good soul, she might oblige."

Madame was only too glad to go, but she was outraged at Julie. Imagine a mother who wouldn't even go with her daughter to such an important event! But Madame said nothing of her thoughts to Sarah and tried instead to smooth away the hurt look on the girl's face as they walked along the busy streets.

"I'm sure you know your part very well, dear, and you will be accepted as a student. What did you prepare for the audition?"

"I've learned the part of Agnes in *Les Femmes Savantes*, by Molière." She said, her face brightening. This was an adventure. "Here's the way I plan to introduce myself. I'll say, 'My name is Sarah Bernhardt,' then I'll curtsy and say I am reciting the part of Agnes—or should I say, I am playing the part of Agnes?"

They discussed *The School of Women* back and forth until they reached the Conservatoire. By this time Madame Guerard was feeling a little nervous and she wondered why Sarah didn't seem the least bit worried. Didn't she know how many hundreds of young people besieged the Conservatoire every year for a chance to study drama? It was a state school, established by Napoleon in 1812. Many of the teachers were the finest actors from the Comédie Française, the famous theater that was the goal of all actors and the pride and joy of France.

Some of Sarah's careless confidence left her when they opened the Conservatoire doors, walked into the small anteroom, and saw so many girls and young men already waiting. Around each one were grouped parents and friends. The air of tension was so strong that it gripped her in the pit of her stomach. Mothers fussed over their daughters' hair; fathers paced up and down or sat, holding their hats between clenched fingers. Most of the contestants looked frankly terrified. One was crying.

Sarah and Madame Guerard found chairs along the wall. "I think I'm going to be sick," Sarah whispered. "It's so crowded in here and someone's been eating something with vanilla in it. It's so strong." Her lips trembled.

Madame Guerard held the girl's hand tightly and smiled reassuringly at her.

A door opened; all eyes swung to it. A young girl, very red in the face, came out, followed by a man. A name was called. Another girl, large and black-haired, swaggering a little to appear sure of herself, stood up, was patted on the shoulder by her friends, had her collar straightened by her mother, and went into the room. A man followed her in too.

When the door closed behind her, all eyes swung back. Some

of the girls looked furtively at each other, as if they were wondering if they were as pretty, if their dresses looked as nice as the others. A boy sat, staring ahead of him, seeing no one, muttering lines under his breath. Next to Sarah was an exceptionally pretty, sweet-faced blonde girl. She leaned over to say, "My name is Marie Lloyd. What is yours?"

Madame Guerard introduced herself and Sarah.

Then Marie asked, "Who is going to give you your responses? Monsieur Colet is an actor at the Odéon," indicating a man who stood near her, glancing over some papers, "and Papa was lucky enough to get him to come today to act with me and give me my responses."

Responses? Madame Guerard and Sarah looked at each other in consternation.

"What does she mean?"

"Oh Sarah, this is terrible! Why didn't someone think of this for you? Of course you have to have an actor play opposite you. You can't just recite Agnes' lines in the play. They are meaningless, as acting, unless you are talking to someone and being answered by someone, as it would be in a real play. Why didn't your mother give some attention to the matter and find out how these examinations are conducted? Why didn't I?" Madame blamed herself harshly, especially when she saw the sick fear in Sarah's eyes.

"Is it absolutely necessary to have someone to give these responses?" Sarah asked Marie Lloyd.

"Oh, I'm sure of it." was the reply. "Papa was instructed that I must have someone in the examination room with me. And, of course, the better actor you have with you, the better you appear to the judges."

Sarah's hands were like ice. What was she going to do? She couldn't go in here alone. In despair, she said to Madame Guerard, "I won't go in there and have them think me a fool. I can't play the part of Agnes with no one to play it opposite me."

"Of course not. You can try again next year. I think it would be much better to do that than to have to make apologies to them and have them send you away. You just sit here. I'll go over to

27

that attendant and tell him Mademoiselle Bernhardt is ill; she is sorry she can't——"

At that moment the door opened. The black-haired girl came out, smiling at the actor with her. Then another man came out and stood in the doorway.

"Mademoiselle Sarah Bernhardt!" he called.

"Don't go, Sarah. I'll explain—" Madame Guerard whispered hurriedly.

For a second the girl sat there. Then, taking a deep breath, she stood up, looked down at Madame with a desperate face, let go of her hand, and walked into the other room.

⁜{ 3 }⁜

The room Sarah walked into was actually the exquisite little theater of the Conservatoire. She entered it from the back and walked down a sloping aisle between the rows of red velvet seats, following an usher who proceeded at a brisk, no-nonsense pace. So hurried was she that she had only a confused impression of tiers of boxes rising up on the two sides of the walls, their railings of pale green painted wood. In front of her was the stage.

The usher led her to one side of it. They passed by men who were grouped in the front rows. Then she was climbing the side steps that led to the top of the high stage. She was standing in the center of it, alone, looking down at upturned faces which were a blur to her.

She curtsied, then said in a voice that was a childish tremble, "My name is Sarah Bernhardt." She swallowed the hard lump in her throat and struck out bravely. "I will recite 'The Two Pigeons,' by Fontaine."

She felt the stir her announcement had caused among the men down below her. She was about to begin the lovely poem when one of the men stopped her. "But why a fable? Haven't you learned a role in a play?"

A silver-haired man answered for her. "Why not a fable? After all, it isn't as long as a whole scene!"

The men laughed. They had a long day ahead of them, listening to so many auditions. Sarah hated them for their laughter but she felt a surge of relief; the silver-haired man had, in effect, given her permission to continue and to substitute the fable for a play.

She began again. It was lucky that she knew the poetry by heart so well that she could have said it in her sleep, because it seemed to her she *was* asleep. She was afraid, so shaking, that she was only half conscious.

"Louder, louder—!" called a little man with curly hair.

She began to cry.

The curly-haired man admonished her impatiently. "Go on, go on. We aren't ogres."

With that she became so angry that she forgot to be afraid. They kept interrupting her and then telling her to go on! How dared they make fun and laugh and be impatient with a poor girl standing up there alone, shivering with fright, trying to do her best? She sraightened her back, threw up her head, tossing her thick mane of hair out of her eyes, and began at the very beginning of the poem.

This time her voice rang out clear and strong. No one interrupted her. All the emotion she was feeling, the desperation, the anger, the intensity of her nervousness, came out in her voice. It was hardly suitable to a light and amusing bit of poetry but it was passionately moving.

So much so that when she finished one man clapped his hands and then stopped abruptly, as if the action had been jolted out of him and he was surprised at himself.

A bell tinkled. Instinctively Sarah knew this was the signal for her to come down off the stage. She managed to bow but she had to hold on to the sides of the stairs as she descended, her knees were shaking so much. Now she could see the men clearly as she faced them on the theater floor. One she recognized, Monsieur Auber, whom she had met several weeks ago when she came for her application.

He smiled at her. "Well, my little woman, it was very good." He indicated the men sitting next to him. "Here are Monsieur Beavallet and Monsieur Provost, who want you in their classes. Which do you prefer?"

It was Beavallet who had interrupted her. It was the silver-haired Monsieur Provost who had said, "Why not a fable?"

"Monsieur Pr– Provost." she stammered.

"Very well." The men turned back to the papers in front of them. The usher tapped her on the shoulder. She followed him, but as she went up the aisle she heard, as in a dream, someone say, "No stage presence at all, of course, but her voice is most unusual. Very musical."

Madame Guerard met her just outside the door. "Well?" she asked, grasping Sarah's arm.

Suddenly Sarah realized what had happened. She had been accepted! She had been picked to enter the Conservatoire. All of her exhaustion left her in one great wave of excitement. "I've been accepted! They liked me!" she cried. "Hurry, please! Let's not walk home, let's hire a carriage. I can't wait. I want to be home when Mama comes. I'm so anxious to tell her. She will be pleased, won't she?" She was babbling and she didn't care as they hurried out of the door and signaled to a hansom cab waiting for a fare.

Madame Guerard fought down a twinge of jealousy. Always it was her mother's approval that Sarah yearned for. Why not? Madame asked herself. Isn't it one of the things I admire in her, this loyalty and devotion, no matter how poor a mother Julie is to her?

When Sarah told her the news, Julie's reaction was only one of unflattering astonishment. She had never believed for one moment that this ugly duckling of hers would be accepted by the Conservatoire.

Fortunately Sarah was too excited to be hurt by her mother's lack of enthusiasm. All thoughts of becoming a nun had vanished.

Here was a new challenge. Classes started immediately and she was busier than she had ever been in her life.

To her shock, the classes were especially hard for her. The Duc might think she was a good mimic, but compared to most of the other students she was not. There were girls there who could copy the actions and looks of anyone they saw. There were boys who could change their expressions in a fraction of a second from the long droop of despair to the glittering eye of rage, or to the sentimentality of love. She was different. Unless she could make herself actually feel the rage or the sentiment or the despair she couldn't make her face do anything; it just kept on looking like Sarah Bernhardt at sixteen years of age.

For her it seemed to be always: "Mademoiselle, please! You are supposed to be feeling anguish over the death of your little son. You look as if you were worrying over which bun to have with your tea. Please let me have some feeling!"

Or: "Mademoiselle Bernhardt, open your eyes wide and smile with delight when you see the man you love coming toward you. Don't look at him with your eyes closed into slits as if you were going to pounce and bite him."

Worse still was the class taught by Monsieur Epie, an elderly actor with elegant gestures and dainty ways, whose false teeth chattered so that Sarah could hardly keep from laughing when he spoke. But his classes were no laughing matter for her.

"Forward, Mademoiselle. The body thrown back, the head high, feet pointed—now walk down these steps and do *not* look at your feet."

She tried but she was tall and awkward. Her long, thin legs would not let her trip along merrily or flow gracefully. Some of the other girls had graceful bodies whose bones seemed to be oiled, like her friend Marie Lloyd. When Sarah went down the steps she couldn't help stealing a peek now and then from under her lashes to be sure that her feet were on the steps and she wouldn't fall. Monsieur Epie caught her doing it, and even with his teeth chattering he was so reproachful she never did it again.

In his class they marched to his "one, two, three—one, two, three." They walked. They turned. They learned to go out of a

31

room with dignity, with nonchalance, or to stalk out with injured feelings. Then it was: "Now, Mademoiselle, leave the room with despair. Your husband does not love you, you have discovered. You do not say a word. It is all to be in the look. In the look, Mademoiselle Bernhardt! That was not the look of despair, it was the look of one terrified by a snake."

How to stand. How to walk. How to sit. Oh, the sitting! Over and over again that reduced Sarah to tears. It was so complicated. It was necessary to meet the seat without a bump, gracefully, without looking behind her, without wondering if the chair was really there or if she would end up on the floor; to go on speaking her lines as she sank down, trying not to wonder also if her skirts were pulled down or her ankles twisted awkwardly.

She took fencing. At first it was torture. Her elbows and knees always seemed to be jutting out at the wrong angles, her foil or *epée* would never go where she wanted it to. Other girls looked pretty in the exercises but she only looked savage, hacking away blindly, her hair falling into her face, perspiration beading her forehead. The only thing the fencing master could compliment her on was her determination. She kept at it long after other girls had collapsed weakly into the nearest chairs.

"Lunge, lunge, thrust in *quart*—march, march, sit, sit—I do them in my sleep," she said to Madame Guerard.

"Are you sure you aren't working too hard? You are getting thinner if that is possible." They were in her apartment and she moved slightly in her chair and put down her knitting so that the girl could lean back against her knees from her favorite cushion on the floor.

"No," Sarah said wearily. "It's all necessary. At first I thought it was foolish. It seemed to be unfair for them to be always making me do things when I looked ridiculous. But Monsieur Provost explained. He said that the fencing not only will give me coordination of muscles. But suppose I were in a scene of a play where I had to suddenly leap over a wall or dash to the other side of the room? Fencing gives you that instantaneous command of your muscles so that they act almost before you think. Or it's

32

supposed to," she added dolefully, rubbing the leg she had bumped against the wall of the *salle d'armes* that day.

Then her face lit up with excitement. "Shall I tell you something nice for a change? Monsieur Samson says my voice is unusual. He examined my throat today because he thought it must have a strange formation. No matter how high or low I speak the words always come out clearly. I don't slur them or shrill them or make them guttural and I always know I can go still higher or lower if I want and not come to the end of my breath. He couldn't find anything different about my throat or mouth."

She helped herself to a pear from the bowl of fruit on the table. "Then he had me recite a poem. He was so pleased—for a moment . . ." Her face fell. "Then he got angry and said why couldn't I put that much emotion into my acting? Sometimes I wish I didn't have any other teachers except Monsieur Provost. He never gets angry with me." She bit the pear. "I tried to tell Monsieur Samson that I could feel what the poem was about but not always what plays are about."

Madame stroked her head. "What did he say then?"

"That that was the difference between an actress and an ordinary person. Anyone can cry when he is hurt, but an actress has to cry when the character she is playing is hurt, not herself."

Even with a large bite of pear in her mouth, Madame Guerard thought to herself, she still sounds as beautiful as music.

"Go to bed now. It's late and you're tired," she said.

"Oh, I can't go to sleep for at least another two hours. I have to study the origins of the theater in Greece." Sarah got up, stretched, yawned, said good night, and left. As she went down the stairs to her mother's apartment she remembered her lessons. Holding her chin high, gathering the folds of her skirt with one hand, she tried to drift down the stairs with regal dignity.

Madame Guerard heard the crash and stuck her head out the door. "Sarah! Are you all right?"

"I'm fine." The words came from down below at the bottom of the steps. The voice was half crying, half giggling. "I fell, but don't tell Monsieur Epie."

It was to Monsieur Provost that Sarah turned for help. It was his influence that kept her in the Conservatoire when she was ready to quit after the first few weeks. It was he who gave all the classes, all the work, a meaning for her.

With him she had individual coaching for the play she must present to the judges at the end of the year. That was all he was supposed to do, but he found in this one student such an eager mind that he prolonged their sessions together and poured some of his own great love of the theater and some of his own intellectual fervor into her.

"Our art, Mademoiselle," he would say as the two rested after a rehearsal, "can be said to have begun with the ancient Greeks. The theater as we know of it can be traced to such geniuses as Sophocles, Aristophanes, and Euripedes. The theater was banned through part of the Middle Ages, then revived with religious plays. Then, slowly came the plays about nonreligious subjects. There were strolling bands of players to amuse the people; special troupes to amuse our French courts.

"But the kind of acting," he continued, smiling at Sarah with his gentle humor, "that I *try* to teach you—for that we can thank Molière. He was the first to make acting natural and real: real subjects, real people. Did you know that he would frequently act with his back turned to the audience if he felt the play demanded that?"

"With my acting, I think the audiences might prefer to have my back turned to them so they couldn't watch me," Sarah said ruefully.

He leaned forward in his chair. He was not well and his face was lined, but his eyes were patient and understanding, glowing darkly under his silver hair. "Don't be impatient. Some of the other students can imitate, which you can't. I'm not sure that this ability to imitate is a good thing. The expression on your face must come from the emotion you feel inside of you and your intelligence. Why intelligence? Because you can never expect to experience in real life all the parts you will play on the stage. You may have to be a miser, a woman who has killed her husband, an Oriental slave, or a shabby little shopgirl going to prison because she has stolen ten francs.

"How do we actors do this? Read, Mademoiselle! Read everything you can about every age, every country, every kind of person in every situation. Observe people around you. Watch what happens to them under emotional strain. Then use your imagination. Close your eyes and imagine you are the person you want to portray. Frighten yourself. Horrify yourself. Be in love—be in pain—want something with all your soul: cry for it, laugh about it. Develop a sensitivity to emotion. The average person trains himself not to show emotion but to smother it. You must do the opposite. Coldness in an actor is fatal. I wouldn't waste my time with you, Mademoiselle, if I thought only that you are intelligent, which you are. I think, too, that you have great capacity to feel.

"You will know, Sarah, that you are an actress when, someday, something very strange happens to you. All you have read about the character you are to portray, all you have thought about her, all that you have carried about her into your dreams as well as your waking thoughts—all this suddenly combines to produce a sum total that is greater than any of these parts. And you *are* that character."

He stood up to show that the lesson was over. "But you are going to have to work harder than you ever believed it was possible for a human being to work."

She did. She worked not only at school but at home, every hour she wasn't eating or sleeping—and even in her dreams. The first year went by swiftly. From a very poor start, Sarah jumped ahead of most of the other students. Monsieur Samson took over her coaching since Provost became ill; he was amazed at her progress. Even Monsieur Epie was impressed by her earnestness. She was not the best in her class but at the end of the first year, in July of 1861, she won a second prize for tragedy and an honorable mention for comedy.

The second year began. Classes resumed. There was much more individual tutoring for each student, though the old classes went on and new ones in Spanish and English were added.

"Now we have to learn to *fall!*" Marie Lloyd said in despair. "I have bruises all over me."

"I know, but when you've taken poison and you're dying at the end of the last act, you'll need to know how to fall or an audience will laugh at you. Look at me. I'm black and blue. At least you are plumper than I and you have something to fall on," Sarah said.

"And you're so brave about it. The rest of us try to fall the easiest way, but you just let yourself go, full length. I'm always afraid you'll be really hurt." Marie was as sweet as she was beautiful. She had come to have great admiration for Sarah; she was awed that anyone would work so hard. Her own grace was a natural one, but she saw that Sarah was acquiring a special, distinctive grace that set her off from the others.

Indeed, now when Sarah walked or came down a staircase Monsieur Epie didn't know whether to applaud or scold. It was a beautiful motion but it wasn't what he had meant to teach her. It wasn't pretty or light or bouncy. Monsieur Epie was a timid little man. He was used to teaching kittens, not panthers.

The fateful day of the second-year public examinations arrived. Each student must act in two plays and be judged on the performances, one in comedy and one in tragedy. Only the best students, those who won the prizes, would be chosen to go to the Comédie Française. Those who were not chosen might try again another year or go to some small, obscure theater of no reputation.

Sarah knew her parts well. It seemed to her that her chances of a first or a second prize were quite good. Unfortunately her mother, who had been quite uninterested in Sarah's two years in the Conservatoire, decided to take her daughter in hand that day. On the morning of the examination she dragged Sarah to her own hairdresser.

"Do something with that unruly, disorderly mop of hair." Julie told him. "She simply cannot stand up in front of people looking like that."

Sarah protested. She had eaten no breakfast because of nerves, and now the smell of hot curling irons and scented oils and creams in the hairdresser's salon was making her ill. Her mother insisted.

"You just put yourself in this man's hands and do as he says. I'm sorry I can't come to the performance to watch you, but at least I have the satisfaction of knowing I've done my best to see that you look nice." She left.

For an hour and a half the hairdresser worked over her hair. It was agony for Sarah, torture to her nerves. It didn't help to hear the hairdresser muttering to himself, "What hair! It is horrible. My God! What hair!" She gritted her teeth and held to the chair with clenched hands. She was pleasing Mama; only this thought sustained her.

When at last he handed her the mirror she was horrified. He had wound the great mass of her tarnished-gold hair into small, individual sausage rolls all over her head. They stuck out. She looked like a porcupine.

It was late. She had to run through the streets to reach the Conservatoire. As she walked to the backstage area the other students gaped at her with their mouths open; some couldn't help but burst into loud shouts of laughter. In the dressing room, before her mirror, it was even worse than she had thought. She broke down and wept.

Marie Lloyd ran in after her. "But what have you done to your hair, Sarah? Your beautiful hair! I've always envied it because it was so soft and silky and you could do so many things with it— pile it up or change it into any style you wanted with a pin or two. Why have you done this?"

While Sarah wept and tried to explain, the two girls pulled out all the sausage rolls and tried to brush it into its natural curls. It was hopeless. The hairdresser had done his work too well. Now it looked like nothing on earth but a tangled bush with prickly, spiky ends sticking out.

While she was still crying, while her eyes were still red and swollen and her voice hoarse with the sobs that had torn her throat, she was called to go on stage. Four hours later the examinations were all over and the prizes were announced.

Sarah Bernhardt's name was not even mentioned, not for any credit whatsoever.

She went to bed that night sick with despair. Two years of work had gone for nothing. She had finished the courses at the Conservatoire and now there was no future for her, no job, no chance for the Comédie Française. Marie had won a first in comedy and the whole Lloyd family was celebrating her success that evening.

Sarah's reception at home had been her mother's shrug and her remark that she really hadn't expected Sarah to do well.

She had just fallen into a fitful sleep when there was a tap on her door. She struggled back into wakefulness. "Yes?"

"May I come in, Sarah?" It was Madame Guerard. "I know how exhausted you are, but I couldn't wait. A message has come for you, delivered by mistake to me. It is from a Monsieur Camille Doucet. He wishes to advise Mademoiselle Bernhardt that due to her fine showing of work all this year she has received special consideration and has been accepted by the Comédie Française."

For a second Sarah just sat upright in bed, staring at the kind, plain face of her friend. Camille Doucet was a dramatist, a man of reputation and influence. If he said—was it possible? It must be true, she was accepted, she was hired . . .

Sarah sprang out of bed. "Oh, do you know what this means? I am to act at the Comédie Française. I'm not a student any more. I haven't failed. The finest theater in all of France, in all the world!"

"Go back to bed this instant. You'll freeze. No, I won't stay and you must get some sleep. We'll talk about it in the morning." Madame Guerard kissed her quickly and was gone.

Instead of going to bed Sarah walked over to the window and stood looking out at the night sky, the chimneypots on the roofs, the sleeping city below. It was a black night, without a star. But not for me, Sarah thought. For me it's a night full of stars and light and brilliance, the happiest, most important night of my life. I am an actress.

{ 4 }

At first the Comédie Française was everything she had dreamed it would be. She went the next morning to sign her engagement and was formerly welcomed by Monsieur L'Administrateur,

Eduoard Thierry. She and Marie, both feeling timid and strange, wandered through the narrow, beautiful halls upstairs that were covered with pictures of the great tragedians and comedians who had acted here. They halted before a bust of Molière.

"New *pensionnaires?*" a voice behind them asked. "I knew you were *pensionnaires;* I can spot that look on your faces. Allow me to introduce myself. I am Monsieur the Stage Manager, Davenne. You are looking at Molière, I see, but did you know this is called 'The House of Molière'? That is because it was he who first broke with the old traditions and brought realism to the French stage. From him we have risen to our present position of the finest theatrical performances in the world."

From her reading Sarah knew quite well that England might say the same of Shakespeare, but she held her tongue. She only said, "Monsieur Thierry said we could go backstage. Would you show us the way, Monsieur Davenne?"

"Certainly. But may I advise you? It is the custom here—I don't know why—to address all officials by their titles, not by their names. It is Monsieur L'Administrateur, not Monsieur Thierry."

With the stage manager as their guide, they walked backstage and saw a rehearsal room, a cavernous place, where actors might work if the stage were occupied. There was a large cleared area in the center, but around all the walls were stage props: tables and chairs, Grecian pillars, a throne, swords hanging from the walls, a simple iron bedstead, an Egyptian mummy propped in one corner, tall Chinese vases, and so much more that Sarah was bewildered.

A man walked by carrying a blonde wig in his hand. The stage manager spoke briefly to him, then returned to the girls.

"That was our wig-maker. His father and grandfather before him made wigs for the Comédie Française. His son and grandson will do the same. It is true also of those who make our costumes. They feel as much a part of the Comédie Française as do the actors. You have no idea of the lengths to which a costume-maker will go to get precisely the right kind of silver button that a noble-man of a certain house, in a certain period, would have worn on a particular riding jacket. To them the study of these things is an art in itself."

He led them down some steps to the stage. It was empty. There was no matinee that day. They walked out onto its bare boards and faced the silent, dim and dusky theater.

"Since sixteen-eighty, when King Louis the Fourteenth brought Molière's troupe and the company of the Hôtel de Bourgogne together to form the national theater of France, the Comédie Française, there has scarcely been an evening or an afternoon when those seats have not been filled to watch a performance here," he said softly. It was perfectly clear to the two girls that the magnificent history of the theater was very dear to him.

Sarah felt it too. She stood on the stage and for a moment it wasn't bare. It was crowded with vivid scenery and the faces of all the famous people who had acted here. There was awe in her soul and a strange, prickling sensation behind her eyelids. She looked out at the rows of red velvet seats and the row upon row of boxes and up to the high galleries. It was almost a perfectly round theater. Red velvet and gold-encrusted box fronts swam in front of her eyes; she stared farther up at the great, beautiful painted dome that arched over the theater.

Someday she would be acting on this stage. It didn't seem possible.

Marie touched her arm. "Come on. Monsieur Davenne is going to take us upstairs to the front public rooms and show us the chair which Molière used in *Le Malade Imaginaire* and in which he died, onstage."

Unfortunately the excitement of being a member of the Comédie Française—or, as it was frequently called, the Théâtre Française—died quickly away. Sarah was only a *pensionnaire*, an actress on probation. If she did well, perhaps in a couple of years she might be admitted to the ranks of the *sociétaires* who had twenty-year contracts, shared in the profits of the theater, and helped to run it. Sarah had once or twice been in the dressing room of a *sociétaire* and had been stunned at the lavish way in which each had decorated these rooms to his own taste. But why not? With twenty-year contracts, some longer, these rooms became second homes to the *sociétaires*.

But for Sarah and the other *pensionnaires* there was nothing of this. She didn't mind not having the contract or the brocaded and gilded dressing room. She did mind—she was frantic—at not having enough to do. She was supposed to learn, to watch, to observe. She was given understudy roles and could substitute once in a while in a rehearsal, but not on stage. A small part in a matinee performance of Jean Racine's *Iphigénie en Aulide* was to be her own debut, but that would not take place until September.

As swift as had been her phenomenal rise at the Conservatoire, when she had gotten her teeth into real hard work, just as swift was her descent here into boredom, indifference, and slackness with so little to occupy her mind.

"But we're not ready yet for big parts," Marie protested, baffled that Sarah should not be as enraptured by the Comédie Française as she was. "We have a great deal to learn. Just think of the privilege it is for us to watch them rehearse; how much we learn from it. They are so kind and helpful to me."

"To you, yes. Not to me. I annoy them. I ask too many questions. I fidget too much. I can't help it, just sitting there in a corner watching other people work. I feel as if I'm going to burst unless I have something to do myself. I even envy the stagehands because they can carry scenery around and I just sit."

There was a brief flare of excitement when she began rehearsing for *Iphigénie*, but it died quickly because her part was so small, her lines so few. When the day of the performance came she spoke and acted without any of the drive of spirit and mind that Monsieur Provost would have demanded of her. The next day Francisque Sarcey, the most prominent theater critic, wrote of her:

Mademoiselle Bernhardt, who made her debut yesterday in *Iphigénie*, is a tall and pretty young person with a willowy waist and a very agreeable physiognomy. The upper part of the face, particularly, is remarkably beautiful. She holds herself well and pronounces her words perfectly distinctly. That is all that can be said of her at the moment.

Sarah read it and squirmed. She went for a long walk to try to cool her bitter, heated thoughts. Not one word in it about her acting! *'That is all that can be said of her'*—well, it was true. She hadn't acted. She had walked through her part. Oh, she hated the Comédie Française and she hated herself for having this turbulent nature, which was always demanding something more and something new.

Passing a shop window, she caught sight of herself. Francisque Sarcey had called her pretty and had said the upper half of her face was beautiful. That was a startling statement. No one had ever said that of her before. She studied her face in the window, jostled by people passing on the sidewalk and hardly noticing them. She turned her chin sidewise, up and down, then looked at herself full-face. Perhaps if she didn't have that low collar, which showed the bones below her neck, and if she weren't wearing these hideous puffed sleeves—Sarah's eye was caught by a model of a dress in the window.

Now that is something more like it, she thought, studying the high, flared collar. The name on the window was MLLE. BERTHE, MODISTE. I'll just go in and have a word with Mademoiselle Berthe.

At the theater she was given two more small parts, nothing at all to use up even a little of the restless fire inside her. To have something to do, she began to think a lot about clothes. Mademoiselle Berthe designed to Sarah's instructions dresses that were strikingly original: strong blues and greens and blacks to show off her creamy skin and tawny curls; long, sweeping, sheathlike skirts that made her look even slimmer and taller; stand-up collars, flaring collars, or cascades of lace under her chin; and always a touch of contrasting color or lace at her wrists to call attention to her very lovely hands.

It was something to do, but not enough. She was so choked up with unreleased energy that she found herself losing her temper over trifles or weeping for no reason at all. She was heading straight for trouble.

And it came on January 15 of the next year, 1863. This was the annual ceremony to celebrate the birth of Molière; his bust was placed in the center of the stage and after the regular play was finished the audience stayed to watch all the members of the company come two by two to place palm leaves in front of it.

Sarah was waiting backstage in the wings for her turn to go on. Just in front of her was Madame Nathalie, an older actress, very stout and at the moment very concerned with how her new velvet evening gown looked on her.

A child standing nearby thoughtlessly stepped on Madame Nathalie's velvet train. The *sociétaire* turned and angrily pushed the child so that she fell against the wall and cut her head. Something exploded in Sarah and she cried out, "You nasty beast!" and slapped Madame Nathalie's face as hard as she could.

Immediately there was an uproar backstage. Madame Nathalie fainted. People rushed around, trying to revive her, trying to keep the procession moving onto the stage, trying to quiet the hysterical Sarah, scolding her for being so violent when the older woman had really meant no harm to the child. The important ceremony was delayed by ten minutes while all this was going on.

The next day Sarah was told: apologize to Madame Nathalie. She replied by tearing up her *pensionnaire* contract in little pieces in front of Eduoard Theirry, dropping the scraps onto his desk, and stalking out. She was through with the Comédie Française.

Unluckily, because she had no time to realize the seriousness of what she had done, she was soon hired by the Gymnase Théâtre who happened to be in need of a young actress, not too well trained so that she wouldn't demand much money, and with a good voice. She had a fairly good part in a fairly good play; she was rehearsing and working every day; it seemed to her to have been an excellent stroke of good business to have left the Comédie Française.

She especially felt this when it was announced one day to the Gymnase company that the Emperor, Napoleon III, had invited some of the actors to the palace to entertain him! And especially when the manager asked her to go because she recited poetry so beautifully. He didn't ask her what she would recite; he would leave that up to her. He was much too excited by this great honor which seldom came to so small a theater as the Gymnase.

43

On the night of the command performance Sarah hired a carriage to take her to the Palais des Tuileries. She gave her name to a splendidly uniformed attendant, who conducted her solemnly to the private chambers of Napoleon and the Empress. As they passed through corridors hung with tapestries, decorated with centuries of the highest skill of silver-worker and goldsmith, furnished with the most magnificent of carved and gilded, enameled and jeweled tables and mirrors, she wanted to pinch herself.

Turning through yet another gorgeous apartment, Sarah suddenly had a quick vision of herself at four, a dirty little street urchin playing in the mud of Paris. If little Titine could see her now! She was never so glad that she had become interested in fashions: her new violet-blue satin gown was very becoming. She could almost feel she had a right to be here.

As the attendant proceeded her into a large room fitted out in yellow brocaded chairs and yellow velvet curtains, she saw the Emperor and Empress seated in two chairs on a slightly raised dais, their personal staff of noblemen and ladies surrounding them.

Her name was announced. She made a deep and graceful curtsy. The Emperor spoke a few words of greeting; the Empress thanked her kindly for coming. Then the difficult moment was over and she was free to join the members of the Gymnase who were standing a little apart at the other end of the room. Almost at once, since she was the last to come and they had been waiting for her, the performance started.

Sarah always had a bad moment of stage fright before going on in a play, but she was never nervous when she had to recite or read poetry. It seemed the most natural thing in the world to do.

When her turn came she moved out to the center of the room and said, "Your Majesties, ladies and gentlemen——"

They were all smiling at her.

"—I shall recite for you a poem by Victor Hugo called 'Oceano Nox.' "

She began to recite and most of her attention was on the words of the poem, but she noticed that Napoleon had abruptly stopped smiling. She heard a startled exclamation, one of horror. Something seemed to be wrong but she didn't know what it was.

How was she, so immersed in the theater, to know anything of politics at her age? How was she to know that Napoleon III had banished Victor Hugo from France for his seditious treasonable writings? That the great author was in exile because he was fond of writing sympathetically of the sufferings of the poor, of writing harshly of weak and corrupt rulers?

She went on, earnestly trying to put more and more beauty into Victor Hugo's poem. She ended. How strange it is they don't applaud, she thought, but perhaps royalty doesn't applaud for poetry. Or perhaps they were waiting for the second poem since it had been announced that she would recite two.

Silence was complete in the room as she bowed and gave the name and the author of the second poem. This one, too, was by Victor Hugo.

It was too much. The Emperor arose, gave his arm to his lady and they swept out of the room in all their outraged royal dignity. The court followed.

The director of the Gymnase rushed up to Sarah where she stood alone in the center of the room, stunned by the withdrawal, and screamed at her in rage: "You have ruined us, you imbecile! Our theater's chance for prominence, for royal approval, and you spoil everything by your stupidity. To recite Hugo—you must have been mad! You——"

A quiet voice interrupted him: "Kindly leave that child alone."

The director wheeled around. Both he and Sarah saw a young man, who from his clothes and his manner, was obviously a member of the royal party. He had lingered behind the others. Now his command hung in the air over the three of them.

The director's fury drove him beyond all prudence. "Why don't you mind your own business, sir? First of all, who *are* you?"

The young man smiled at Sarah. That smile touched something in her heart that had never been touched before. He said, "I will not allow a woman to be insulted in my presence. I am Prince Henri de Ligne."

[5]

"So I explained to their Majesties that you meant no insult in reciting Hugo, that you knew nothing of his being banished. They have forgiven you. Has the director given you any more trouble?" It was a week later. The prince and Sarah were strolling through the wooded paths of the Bois de Boulogne at that time of evening when Paris seems to be illuminated by its own special shimmery gray-blue light.

"No." Sarah laughed. "You frightened him. Besides, we are in the midst of rehearsals and it would be difficult to replace me now."

So much had happened in one week. The most important thing was that she was in love with Prince Henri; the most incredible thing was that he loved her too. She could hardly believe it. He had escorted her home from the palace that evening and had called for her every day at the theater.

"Chilly? No?" He slipped her hand into the crook of his arm and held it there as they walked. He was tall and handsome, scarcely older than she, though his dignity made him seem older. This walking about in a public park was a new thing for him, the sort of ordinary thing that ordinary people did. He was enjoying it because Sarah was with him and everything Sarah did was exciting. She made other girls look like stupid dolls. She was vibrant, alive; she brought adventure into the boring routine of his life. "Are you positive you would not like to stop in a café and have a hot drink to warm you?"

"I'm too happy to sit still. I'd run on that lawn over there if it wouldn't shock people; I'd run and dance. Oh, I wish I didn't

46

have to go home so soon but if I'm tired tomorrow I won't be able to play my role. Henri, after we are married, I shall only play when there is some special part that interests me."

She felt his arm stiffen and there was a moment's hesitation before he said, "Yes, Sarah. After—after we are married."

But she was too happy to think that anything was strange. The mystery of the early-evening shadows was all around them. The very thinnest and finest of mist was sprinkling her hair with drops that glittered like tiny jewels under the flicker of the gas lamps. The radiance in her eyes as Prince Henri drew her into the darker shadows of a tree to kiss her was so bright that it touched his heart with wonder and surprise.

"Yes, Sarah," he murmured, this time with conviction, "after we are married you shall do just as you please."

After we are married . . .! In her own room that night she said the words over and over to herself. She had no one to confide in. Madame Guerard was visiting relatives. Sarah had no wish to tell her mother about Henri or that she was in love with him, knowing the kind of questions her mother would ask about money and position and so forth.

It was tragic that Sarah was so young, so innocent, so unsophisticated, so completely alone without anyone to guide her at that moment.

The next few months were ones of wild, wonderful happiness for her. The play at the Gymnase was a mild success and the director was pleased with the spirit she threw into her acting. Every afternoon she met Henri and they went for a ride or a walk; every evening he called for her after the performance.

What happened was inevitable. The wonderful dream she was living in crashed around her feet.

"Marry you? A prince? Of course he won't marry you! You've been the worst kind of a fool." Her mother was furious. "And where is your precious Henri now, may I ask?"

"He is away on a trip. He had to go. But he said he wanted to marry me. He does," Sarah sobbed. "He's good and honorable, he loves me——"

"Oh, stop that sniffling. You had better be thinking of what to do, or I suppose I must. You will have to leave the city for a while. But don't expect me to support you and your child when you come back."

After her mother had rustled indignantly out of the room, Sarah lay on her bed, trying desperately to think and not to cry. She was sure Henri loved her as much as she did him—but she also remembered how his arm had stiffened when she had mentioned marriage, how awkward had been his hesitation. Her mother must be right; she was a sophisticated woman. Henri was gone and she must do what her mother told her to.

Sarah resigned from the Gymnase and went to Spain. Her son was born. Several months later she brought him back to Paris and found a tiny, shabby two-room apartment for herself and the baby.

She had to work now for someone besides herself, someone she loved with all the love in her soul. Just looking at the helpless infant asleep in his crib and knowing that little Maurice was dependent upon her for everything, for life itself, had wrought a great change in her. No longer was she the same self-absorbed, careless, thoughtless girl she had been.

She was twenty years old. Bitterly now she regretted the foolish impulse that had made her tear up her Comédie Française contract. With that she would have been safe and Maurice would have been safe, instead of living this half-starved existence on the few francs she borrowed from her mother.

The word had gone around the theatrical circles that Sarah Bernhardt was untrustworthy. She had torn up one contract and left the Gymnase without a week's notice.

"The only engagement offered me," she told Madame Guerard as the two sat sewing clothes for Maurice in Sarah's cramped, ugly little parlor, "is as an understudy. You understand? Not as an actress. But they will give me a small salary to study the part of Princess Desiree just in case the regular actress falls ill or has an accident, so that I would be ready to step in."

"There must be something better than that. Have you seen all the managers, all the theaters?"

Madame Guerard had returned to Paris, heartbroken over Sarah's tragedy. She did not blame the girl for her mistake. What else was to be expected when Sarah had found love for the first time, when she had never had the benefit of a mother's love or wisdom or guidance? But Madame Guerard resolved, within herself, that henceforth she would do everything she could to help this girl. She couldn't give her money because Madame was too poor, but she would do everything else she could.

"I must take the job. I have to pay a girl to come in every day to take care of Maurice while I'm away. I have to pay rent, somehow. I must find the money to pay Mama back what she has loaned me."

Luck was with her. The actress she understudied did fall ill and Sarah stepped into the part. It was a comic role in an operetta—not at all the sort of thing she liked—but this was no time for temperament. She worked hard and did well. Her name replaced the other woman's on the placards outside the theater door.

It was because of this that Henri was able to find her. There was a knock on her dressing-room door one night and the prince stood there, reproach on his face.

"Where have you been? I have searched for you everywhere. I went to your mother's house but it was boarded up. They told me she had gone for a visit to your Aunt Rosine. If I had not seen your name outside by accident, I might never have known where you were. Why have you been hiding from me?"

"You wanted to find me?" She could hardly believe it, even when he was holding her tightly in his arms. When she told him about their son, the prince was overwhelmed by remorse for what she had gone through alone.

"You were quite right to suspect that I was not serious about marriage. But I am now. While I was away I knew that nothing mattered but being with you."

For weeks Sarah floated on a cloud of hope and joy, made all the more ecstatic because this had come as a reprieve after she had believed herself deserted.

She was in her apartment alone one evening, because the play had finally closed and rehearsals had not yet started for the new one. The doorbell rang and she opened the door expecting to see Henri, but it was a stranger who stood there, a much older man.

"Yes? You wished to see me?" she asked.

"I do, if you are Mademoiselle Sarah Bernhardt. I am General de Ligne, Prince Henri's uncle."

"Please come in, sir." Sarah could tell at a glance that this was not going to be a pleasant meeting, but she ushered him into her poorly furnished room with all the grace of a queen—which seemed to make him feel uncomfortable.

The general was representing the whole de Ligne family. At the news of the forthcoming marriage, a veritable storm had broken out in the de Ligne household. Henri's father, the Prince Eugène, was unable to come so the general had been sent instead to confront the scheming, unscrupulous girl who had tricked Henri into wanting to marry her.

"It is my marriage to Henri that you wish to discuss, is it not?" Sarah asked, her hands clenched behind her back.

"Yes." He sat down heavily, not liking what he had to do. "You must realize how impossible it is. Henri is the last son, the heir of his great and noble line. It is imperative that he marry in his own class and that his children be of a blood to match his own. If he marries you it will be a disgrace to the family. Henri, married to you, will be cut off from all his friends. He will be disowned and penniless, with no hope of a career suitable for him. Do you honestly think his love can survive such misery for him?"

The general had hastily revised what he had planned to say. This was no scheming girl. He would have to appeal to her love for his nephew.

"Do you not think he will grow to hate you and your child for having ruined him?" he added.

She had been about to tell him that neither she nor Henri cared for any of the things he had mentioned, but this last shot struck her deeply. That Henri should come to hate her, that he should drag out a miserable, impoverished existence with her and come to blame and despise her for it—this could not be borne.

She was silent as the older man pursued his point. "He loves you now, but what when he loses his rank, his fortune, his family and friends? What will you have to offer him except a romantic notion that will turn into a burden for him? Isn't it better that the two of you keep the memory of your love and happiness unspoiled? Love changes, my dear. He has not been trained for any kind of work. What will happen to him as a man when he has to live off your earnings? Have you thought about what will happen to him?"

And what will happen to me? Sarah was crying inwardly. What of me?

But she knew the general was right.

"Please go," she managed to say. "I will do as you ask but please leave me alone just now. You needn't worry: I will not tell Henri that you came to see me. He must think the decision is mine alone or he will never agree to it. Hurry—he will be here any moment."

The general left, fingering in his pocket the check he had meant to give her but which he knew she would fling back at him.

When Henri came there was a terrible scene. Sarah told him, coldly, that while she loved him she realized that she was first and always an actress. She would not give up the theater for him, it must always come before anything else with her. It was lucky, she said, that she had come to her senses before it was too late. As the Princess de Ligne she would be unhappy and out of her element. She had a glorious career ahead of her, with managers sending her messages every day to be in their dramas, and she could not give that up for any husband.

Henri at last believed her. "I see. Evidently the stage means more to you than I do. I should have known what you are—cheap, unworthy, a selfish exhibitionist like all actresses who want nothing out of life but to flaunt themselves before the public."

He slammed the door as he left. There was a finality to the sound of it that spelled for Sarah the end of her youth and its sweet, unshadowed dreams. She did not collapse. She did not even cry. That was all over. She went to the window, opened it, and leaned out into the fog-veiled night.

She could see the wet and shining pavement below, lit by the flare of the lamps. Across the street in a fashionable apartment house she could see that a party was going on. There seemed to be hundreds of gleaming candles shining against the crystal of the chandeliers; through the looped draperies of the windows she caught glimpses of beautifully gowned women and the formal attire of the men. Music came faintly to her ears.

What of me? she cried again silently. What am I going to do? What can I give my child?

Sarah took a deep breath. I can give myself, she thought. I'm all he has and I promise with everything I hold sacred that he will never want for anything. Someday I will give him all the money and beauty that I see over there; but right now and forever he will have the mother's love I never had. I'll work for him with all the strength of my body and all the intelligence Monsieur Provost said I had. I'll work until I drop; I'll study and learn; I'll force the managers to give me parts. Someday I'll be rich enough to give him everything and I'll be the kind of actress and mother he'll never he ashamed of.

Now that she was so determined she also began to plan. There was one man, Camille Doucet, the one who had thought so much of her at the Conservatoire that he had helped her get into the Comédie Française. He was now director of the Beaux Arts Théâtre.

The next day she went to see him in his office. She went straight to the point. "I know I have a reputation for being flighty and undependable, but that is all changed. Now I want a long-term contract, terms which will mean the hardest kind of work and which will put penalties on me if ever I try to break away."

He was astounded. This was a new Bernhardt. He was convinced she really meant it.

"Very well," he answered. "If you mean what you say, I have exactly what you are looking for. The management of the Odéon is under my control. I have just hired two new managers—a Monsieur de Chilly and a Monsieur Felix Duquesnal. Felix has seen you act. He mentioned it to me one day and he thinks you are charming and your voice unique. Go to see him; he may approve such a contract."

Monsieur Duquesnal did, over the protests of his partner.

It was now 1866. She had been an actress, so-called, for four years, but in that time she had done very little real acting. Even though her name had appeared several times on billboards outside of theaters, she was just beginning the hard, strenuous work of her career.

The Odéon, where she reported for work that week, was a repertory theater like the Comédie Française, though not with its reputation. It, too, had a regular company of actors and actresses hired on long-term contracts. The classics of Molière and Racine and others were presented nearly every week, usually at matinees; new plays were introduced in the evenings. Sarah's first part was in the Molière play, *Les Femmes Savantes*, and she was certainly no shining star in it. It was the role of a flirt and this kind of cuteness was difficult for her, but she neither pouted nor was sullen and worked as hard and obediently as any director could have wished.

Then came the beginning of the year 1867. The Odéon decided to put on *Athalie* by Racine. Sarah was given the part of Zachariah, a young man.

"Listen carefully, Mademoiselle Bernhardt." Monsieur Duquesnal had taken her aside into the empty wings at the side of the stage. They sat down on an old trunk that held unused costumes. "I am trying an experiment and if it fails I shall be the laughing-stock of Paris for daring to trifle with a play of Racine's. You know the story of *Athalie*?"

He did not wait for her nod but plunged on. Stagehands walked around, moving props, working just behind Monsieur Duquesnal's back, but he paid no attention to them. He was intent on what he was saying. "It is an Old Testament story. Queen Athalie is the widow of the King of Judah whom she hated always because he killed her wicked mother. She hated him and all his line, descending from David, so much she had her own children and grandchildren murdered because they were also the offspring of her husband. An inhuman woman, she was motivated by hatred not only of the late King but of the Lord God of the Jews. She worshipped her own idol, Bael, and forced the Jews to set up the statues of Bael in all public places."

"But," he continued, oblivious to the fact that Sarah knew the story well, "she had not dared to destroy the Temple of the Lord

53

nor the High Priest Jehoida nor his son Zachariah nor the foundling child whom the High Priest had sheltered in the Temple. What she did not know was that the foundling child was actually her grandchild whom Jehoida saved from murder.

"When the play opens Athalie has had a dream of a face of a boy. It troubled her. It was a threat; it was somehow connected with the Temple."

"So she went to the Temple—" Sarah said, but he interrupted her.

"Yes, yes. And she was right." Duquesnal was impatient to get on with the story in his own way, for his own purpose. "The High Priest had saved the boy, hoping the time would come when around him the forces of good could be rallied to fight the forces of evil, as embodied in the Queen . . . Athalie came to the Temple, saw the boy, knew he was the boy in her dream, realized that whoever he was he meant danger to her and must be destroyed. She went away. The Hight Priest knew he must act quickly; the time had come when the people must be told that their new King, their real King, lived and was among them. The High Priest gathered a group of faithful men and hid them in the Temple. When Athalie came again, she was permitted into the sacred inner room of the Temple, confronted by the boy, told who he was—but when she ordered her soldiers to kill the boy, she and her soldiers were surrounded, driven out into the streets, and destroyed by the people."

Sarah wondered why he was taking so much trouble to tell her this. Certainly the part of Zachariah was an insignificant one in the play. Hesitantly she said as much.

Duquesnal nodded. "Ordinarily, yes. That is where I am going to make a radical change. As you know, all through the play there is a chorus usually sung and spoken by Zachariah and the daughters of Levi. This chorus is more than just a poetic addition to the play. It raises the play to nobility and grandeur. But there will be no chorus as we stage it. You, as Zachariah, will not only speak your own lines but also take the place of the whole chorus."

"But why?" One of the actors had joined them in time to hear this last remark of the manager's. "That's never done in *Athalie*."

"I know. Look, the chorus either makes the play sublime or, if it is a poor chorus, destroys the beauty of it. The Comédie Française can afford to hire beautiful girls with good voices and spend the money to train them thoroughly so that their chanting together is a joy to watch and hear. We haven't that kind of money. I could get pretty girls with no voices, probably, or trained singers who are fat and homely. It would be a miracle for me to find both looks and voice with what I can afford to spend. So I am gambling on Sarah and her voice."

He stood up and faced Sarah. "This is a large responsibility for you, Mademoiselle," he said. "You will be surrounded by a group of lovely girls; the daughters of Levi must appear; but you will do all the speaking and singing. I know you aren't a singer; however, the chorus is best done in a kind of lyrical speaking-chant and that you can do. What do you think?"

"I think I should like to try." She smiled at him.

She studied hard, taking her work in two parts. One was the character of the boy, Zachariah. She reread her Old Testament. She read histories of the Jews of that period. She thought about Zachariah: what kind of a boy would he be? Not an ordinary boy surely, raised as he was in the High Priest's dwellings, taught always that his mission in life was to help destroy false gods and bring back to the people their faith in the one God. But he was young. He and the boy King played together. It was a kind of youthful innocence, together with a spiritual sensitivity and bravery, that she must capture, for the part.

Then there was the work of the chorus. All evening long, as she cleaned the rooms of her apartment or cooked her thrifty supper or rocked Maurice to sleep in her arms, she chanted the words of the chorus. The director had wisely decided to let her practice this by herself and he gave her only the slightest advice. Gradually she knew the words of the chorus and the meaning of each line so well that it came to her naturally which words should be spoken slowly for their full effect, which should be chanted, and which required the most musical effect of singing.

55

Little Maurice loved it. The sound of his mother's voice was enchanting to him and he happily gurgled his own accompaniment as he lay in her arms.

{ 6 }

On opening night Sarah peeked through the curtains at the audience. Here, on the Left Bank of the river Seine, there were only a few well-dressed theatergoers. These sat downstairs, only partly filling the lower floor, or were sprinkled through the lower boxes. It was the galleries above which were jammed. Here sat the poor students of the Left Bank universities.

She was frightened with more than her usual stage fright. These students were not well behaved. If they didn't like the performances they were capable of loud boos and jeers and whistles. They had strong feelings about the drama and showed them. If Duquesnal's innovation of one singer trying to be a whole chorus was a failure, these students might get so rowdy they would stop the performance halfway through.

Her heart pounding, she waited. It was not until nearly the end of the first act that she, in her boy's tunic, with her hair fixed so that it seemed to hang short just below her ears, came onto the stage followed by the chorus, to hear her mother say:

> "Dear Zachariah, go, nor stay thy steps,
> "Accompany thy venerable sire. . . .
> "Daughters of Levi, young and faithful band . . .
> "Sing, praise the God whose presence here ye seek."

This was the cue for the chorus to break into song. Instead, this night, the chorus remained silent, sitting in graceful poses behind Sarah. She alone, as Zachariah, stepped forward to chant:

56

"His glory fills the universe sublime . . ."

her voice, pure and sweet, rising gloriously, filled the theater.

"Lift to this God for aye the voice of prayer!"

Hers was not an operatic voice; she spoke the lines as much as she sang them, but the effect electrified the audience. Up in the galleries the students were still; they leaned perilously far over the railings. They were spellbound by that voice. It was tingling their nerves and clutching at their hearts. Below them on the stage, Zachariah was the pure in heart, the young in spirit, the glad beauty of song raised in devotion to God.

When the scene ended and the curtain came down, there was a strange sound all through the darkened theater, a sound of the whole audience expelling its breath in a sigh, a breath that had been held and pent up all during the chorus.

In the next scene she was to act. As Zachariah she must run into the Temple room where the mother was, to cry "The Temple is profaned!" to tell of Athlaie's first visit, to show through Zachariah the awful sacrilege that was committed by the presence of the evil woman in the House of the Lord. It was a long speech and a very intense one, full of the shock and the horror of what had happened.

Sarah stood before the wife of the High Priest. She was panting a little; she had been running. She said the first words, then: "The Temple is profaned!"

At that moment the thing that Monsieur Provost had promised her so many years ago actually happened to her. The blending together of the work of her mind, her imagination, her work—all came together in perfection and worked a kind of magic. She was no longer Sarah Bernhardt. She was Zachariah. She was a boy in Old Testament days, shocked to his very soul by what had happened and what he must tell his mother.

The other actors and actresses felt Sarah's acting as if it were electricity. They had been playing their parts competently and ably, now they rose above themselves to meet her challenge. Her speech became the pivot on which the whole drama turned and became a thing of passion and fire.

And when at the end of that act Zachariah again sang for the chorus:

> "How often, Lord, how often yet shall we
> "Against Thee rising up the wicked see? . . ."

it was more than the students could stand. Her voice had aroused and thrilled them so, her acting had breathed such real life into the play, that they could remain silent no longer and broke into a cheering, stamping, yelling pandemonium.

Downstairs, the more sedate, conservative audience glared up at the galleries and tried in vain to hush them. They could not be stopped until some of their excitement had been worn out. Only then could the play be resumed.

When it was over and the curtain had come down, and had been raised again and again to repeated ovations, the students poured in their usual noisy rout down the stairs, talking enthusiastically to each other of what they had seen:

"I never heard a voice like that! She's marvelous, this what's-her-name—this Sarah Bernhardt!"

"When she said, like that—'The Temple is profaned'—I had goose flesh."

"I broke out in a cold sweat, I tell you. I was shivering all over."

"Ah, but when she sang! That was music, that was beauty."

They came back the next night and brought their friends. The word flashed through the universities, through the students' shabby rooms, through the little cafés where they met. Shrewdly, Duquesnal kept *Athalie* playing for days, though as a rule Racine was no novelty to Paris and managers put on his plays for a day or two just as a matter of prestige for their theaters, or played him once or twice a week at a matinee.

This success at the Odéon was unusual. And when it had to be withdrawn, Duquesnal gave Sarah the role of Cordelia, the good daughter in Shakespeare's *King Lear*. Again she surprised him by the way she created herself "into" the role.

She was living and working the way that Monsieur Provost had taught her, adding to it that which was original and her own. Too poor to buy new clothes for herself, since her slightly larger salary at the Odéon must go for the necessities of living and for paying back, week by week, what she owed to her mother, nevertheless she managed to squeeze out a few francs to buy books when she couldn't borrow them. It was not only the theater she was studying, but actors as well.

She found that the great French actor Talma said:

> When we consider all the qualities necessary to form an excellent tragic actor, all the gifts which nature should have bestowed upon him, can we be surprised that they are so rare? Amongst the majority of those who go on the stage, one has penetration, but his soul is cold as ice. Another possesses sensibility, but intelligence is wanting. One possesses both these requisities, but in so slight a degree, that it is as if he did not possess them at all.

On the other hand other French actors of the past century argued against this and insisted that the actor must not feel his part. Denis Diderot claimed that an actor should rely only on intelligence; if he were a good actor he could portray an emotion without actually feeling it.

Sarah worried over this. She felt that Talma was right. But suppose she were to play the same part night after night, week after week? If she were to rely solely on her own emotions, a night would surely come when she was tired or nervous or it would be impossible to summon up the emotion inside of her. Wasn't there something to be said for intelligence entering into it and the actions and speech conveying an emotion, even if she didn't feel it?

Otherwise, Sarah decided, she would turn into a nervous wreck, going through all the passions of life and death every night.

For most women in their early twenties, this period in Sarah's life would have been so dull they couldn't have borne it. She had no fun, no friends except Madame Guerard, no companionship at home except her baby son, no life outside of the theater and her home. But if it was dull Sarah didn't know it; she had no time to think of herself in this way.

Duquesnal gave her a raise in salary. She moved her few pieces of furniture to a larger apartment because it had a room for a servant to sleep in. Now she could afford a full-time nurse for Maurice and never again would she have to frantically send for Madame Guerard to come and look after her son because the part-time maid announced suddenly that she could not come that particular evening.

For the next year she quietly went her way, acting in any part the Odéon would give her and learning from each one of them. But Duquesnal had his eye on her. He had not forgotten the sensation of her voice in *Athalie*. He was aware that more and more the students were coming to the theater solely to watch and clap for Sarah Bernhardt.

"What next for me, Monsieur?" she asked him one day when it was obvious that the current play would be closing soon.

"I have no part in the next one for you," he told her, watching with amusement the disappointment in her face. "No, not in the play itself. But I have come across the work of a young poet named François Coppée. In my opinion he will someday be one of France's greatest. He has written a poem in the form of a one-act play, with just two characters in it. I intend to put it on in addition to the main drama. It will be something new and different for our audiences."

He picked up a bound manuscript. "Here. Take it home and read it. Mademoiselle Agar will play Sylvia and you will be the minstrel boy, Zanetto."

That night when Maurice woke from his nap and cried to be picked up, she held him in her arms and crooned, not a lullaby, but the lovely words of the poem.

"Such beautiful words!" she told him. "You don't understand them, little one, but even you like the sound of them. See—I will put you here in all these cushions and pillows and you will watch me. Now I am Sylvia, a rich and beautiful Italian lady living on my estate near Florence. It is evening and I am walking on the terrace." She paced slowly down an imaginary path and came to rest her elbows on an imaginary wall, which happened to be the table. The little boy laughed in delight at such antics.

"I am Sylvia and I am bored with too much wealth, too much cynicism in fashion and society and morals. Suddenly I see below me, over the wall, a young man—a boy, really—with a guitar slung over his shoulder, flowers in his hand. He is singing a song. It is Zanetto, the troubador. He has no money, no place to sleep, but he is happy. He lies down on an old bench for the night."

Sarah used the couch for the bench, throwing herself down, but wincing a little as the broken springs dug into her back.

"Now you see, little Maurice, the lovely lady, Sylvia, is intrigued by the cheerful happiness of this boy and by his handsome looks. And because he seems to care not at all that his only bed is a hard bench and his only covering for the night are the stars in the heavens."

The baby boy pushed a pillow off onto the floor, but his round eyes never left his mother as she got up from the couch and once more became Sylvia. "She comes down from the terrace and walks close to Zanetto. She questions him."

In a flash Sarah was once more sitting on the couch, holding her arms around her knees, rocking back and forth in the manner of a charming, laughing, eager boy. "He tells her he is a wanderer, homeless, but he loves his life. He goes where he wants to, sings his songs for his supper, his friends are the stars and the sun, the flowers and the wind. He tells her he is going to Florence in the morning and he has been told of a rich, beautiful lady named Sylvia who might perhaps like his songs."

Sarah moved in stately fashion across one end of the room. The maid stuck her head inside the door from the kitchen, fascinated as always by Mademoiselle's goings-on. The baby was quiet, watching.

"Poor Sylvia," Sarah said softly. "She yearns to have this boy as her page, to keep him with her always so that his songs will amuse her and lighten her heart. But she thinks—just in time— that if she cages this bird he will not be happy. His wings will be clipped, he will fade and die away in captivity, no matter how much gold and silver she gives him."

So sad was her voice that Maurice puckered up his forehead and began to cry. Sarah ran to pick him up and cuddle him. "No, no—it all ends happily. Sylvia tells Zanetto he must not seek out this horrible rich woman Sylvia. He must go on as he always has.

So she sends Zanetto on his way, singing and free and happy, in bondage to no one. Before he goes he asks for a gift. She wants to give him a gold ring, but all he wants is the flower in her hair. Isn't that a nice story?"

Sarah took Maurice and put him onto his little cot beside her own bed. She stood for a moment looking down at him. He's hardly a baby any more, she thought. He's becoming a little boy. And she felt for the moment desperately lonely, remembering the prince. She tried hard not to think of him or the love she had lost, but sometimes she could not help herself.

Then she went back to the sitting room to study Zanetto further. What would he look like? Who could tell her what clothes, what hairdress and costume, an Italian minstrel boy would have worn?

She studied pictures in books and went to art galleries. For hours she paced up and down in front of paintings, studying a page-boy in this one, a musician in that one. Nothing suited until one day she went to an exhibition and saw a statuette called "The Florentine Singer."

Duquesnal was astonished when she described to the costume-maker exactly what she wanted and why. But he saw how right she was when, on opening night Zanetto came on stage walking along the grassy turf toward the old bench, singing of flowers and of April.

A gasp of sheer admiration went up from the audience.

Zanetto was dressed in a tight-fitting costume of light purple, with doublet and hose, and a small white ruff around his neck; a velvet cap with a tall feather in it, a guitar slung over his shoulder. Sarah's figure was charming in the costume. She looked like a boy. And under the cap her face was alive with the sweet joy of living that only the strange, untouched, untamed, unworldly Zanetto would know.

Her voice was never better. It had a lilt of springtime lightness when Zanetto was singing to himself; an eager rapture when he saw and admired the beautiful Sylvia; a hint of puzzled wonder when he felt that Sylvia was holding out promises to him and then rejecting him; of bashful tenderness when he asked for the flower in her hair; of careless, happy, unclouded farewell as he picked up his guitar and strolled off at the end of the play.

Mademoiselle Agar's statuesque, mature beauty was the foil against which the poetry of Zanetto played and danced and sang.

When the curtain closed, the audience cheered until they were hoarse—the lower floor and boxes as well as the students in the galleries. Sarah and Mademoiselle Agar took curtain call after curtain call. For the first time Sarah heard the cries of "Bernhardt! Sarah Bernhardt!" coming from all parts of the house, though naturally the yelling was loudest from the galleries.

It was her first real success. Mademoiselle Agar good-naturedly insisted on Sarah taking many of the curtain calls alone. It was Zanetto, not Sylvia, who was the sensation of the evening.

The newspaper critics mentioned her with praise. Even across the river, into the splendid rooms of the Comédie Française, the report trickled: "Have you heard about Sarah Bernhardt? That girl who slapped Madame Nathalie and tore up her contract? She's had quite a little success at the Odéon."

François Coppée, though he must dedicate Le Passant to the older actress, Mademoiselle Agar, took up much of his dedication in raving about Sarah's performance and her exquisite blonde beauty.

Sarah was startled. She was beginning to think rather well of her voice and her abilities as an actress, but she had never thought of herself as a beauty.

"What you don't realize, Sarah," Madame Guerard told her, "is that you have changed. Those gaunt hollows in your face have filled out, so that where, before, you were so broad across the eyes and cheekbones and so pointed in your chin, now your face is a smooth, long oval."

Yes, Madame thought, watching Sarah examine herself critically in the mirror, the resemblance to a cat is almost gone. I shall miss it. Her eyes are still long and slanted up, but they don't seem quite so odd—just strikingly beautiful. She will never have the rosebud prettiness of her mother, but she has ten times the distinction.

❧ 7 ❧

Le Passant was performed all summer, more than one hundred times. Duquesnal had not planned on this. It was forced on him by popular demand, by people besieging the box office for tickets.

Other theater managers began to take notice of the Bernhardt girl. Offers were made to her, but she kept her promise and respected her contract with the Odéon. When *Le Passant* finished, she went immediately into other plays, some good, some mediocre, but in all of them her own parts were excellently done. Slowly she was building a small reputation in Paris.

The war between France and Germany in 1870 caught her by total surprise since she cared so little at that time for politics. But her instincts and her heart were flamingly patriotic; even when Paris was in danger of being occupied by the enemy, she refused to run away as so many others were doing.

Instead, she looked about her for some way to help her country. All the theaters were closed in this national emergency, so that the Odéon stood empty while the hospitals were overcrowded and wounded men waited their turn to find beds. She had an idea and acted on it: to turn the Odéon into a hospital.

Sarah had no idea what this would mean; she had never been near sickness or pain, wounds and death. But she did not abandon the work. She found to her amazement that she had a knack for the management so desperately needed. Somehow she got beds and bandages that the doctors needed; she maneuvered her friends into acting as nurses; she found drugs and medicine when they seemed impossible to locate. Day and night, going without sleep, Sarah ran her hospital. She forgot she was an actress and remembered only that she was a Frenchwoman.

In 1871 peace came. The theaters slowly reopened. The people of Paris were sick of death and destruction and longed for something to make them forget what they had been through. They wanted lights and color and music and a different kind of drama from the sad one of war. They flocked to the theaters.

The Odéon was renovated. Almost immediately Sarah was handed a fine plum, a leading role in a new one-act play: *Jean-Marie*, by André Theuriet. Then came another in *The Other*, by George Sand. The students were back, the older ones still in soldier uniforms, the younger ones bringing their friends from the universities. It was one of them who first used the word "golden" to describe Sarah's voice. After that it was used constantly, along with everything else the audience and newspaper critics could think of: pure music, ethereal music, the ripple of waterfalls or of harpstrings.

She was the favorite of the Left Bank, but while she appreciated this she knew that the other Paris, the Paris who considered the Comédie Française to be the one and only theater representative of the best, had only just begun to be aware of her existence.

After every performance she searched the pages of *Le Temps*, the newspaper in which Francisque Sarcey wrote. If only he would write about her! This one man was famous for his knowledge of the theater and he had it in the power of his pen to make or break actresses.

Every night he saw a play; he studied drama and the actors; he followed careers with a careful eye. He was ruthlessly honest and bluntly outspoken. He had mentioned Sarah in her debut at the Comédie Française; since then he had hardly noticed her, except for a word of praise for Zanetto in *Le Passant*.

She would have to be more than successful. She would have to be outstanding to truly catch his attention.

It was late in the year 1871 when the managers of the Odéon told Sarah that they were going to put on a revival of *Ruy Blas* by Victor Hugo. The play had been long awaited by the French public; now that Victor Hugo was back from exile and no court had the power to call him treasonous any more, it was time for *Ruy Blas*.

Sarah's role as Doña Maria de Neubourg, the Queen of Spain,

was a major one. For a young woman of twenty-seven to play such a regal part was not easy. Victor Hugo's complex story of political intrigue, noble passions, feuds, and the cross-currents of feudal knightly codes of honor made great demands upon the ability of any actress.

One day at rehearsal the rumor flew from actor to actor: Victor Hugo has come! He is here, in person, in the theater!

All the company tried hard to hide their curiosity and not to stare, to go about the rehearsal as if nothing was happening and one of the greatest men of literature was not walking toward the stage with the managers on either side of him. Victor Hugo was a legend, a hero, a giant among men.

He was introduced to each actor, one by one. As he met Sarah he bowed over her hand and she noticed with awe the fine, high, noble forehead and the clear, calm, and penetrating eyes. "I'm charmed, Mademoiselle. I am happy you will be playing the part of Doña Maria."

He was very polite and courteous but Sarah had a sudden thought that he was really not at all happy about it. If Victor Hugo had a weakness it was that he thought his plays better than his novels, which they weren't. The part of Doña Maria was most important to him; Sarah guessed that he could not believe that one who had been a lighthearted boyish Zanetto could also be a tragically powerful Doña Maria.

He settled himself in a chair to watch the rehearsal.

They were going through the last scene of the last act. The actor who played Ruy Blas approached the Queen where she sat, horror-struck at seeing him kill Don Salluste. Ruy Blas begged forgiveness and pardon but the Queen Doña Maria said, "Never!"

Sarah was looking anything but regal or queenly at the moment. She was dressed in her much-worn black dress, her hair was tumbled because she had a habit of running her hands through it distractedly while she thought of a problem or a bit of action in rehearsals. Yet when she said, "Never!" Victor Hugo raised his eyebrows in surprise. The tone was just right. And the guesture that followed it, as the Queen saw with amazement Ruy Blas take a phial from the table to drink what was in it, was just right too.

Victor Hugo leaned forward. His cape fell to the ground behind him, unobserved. He listened.

Sarah róse and came toward Ruy Blas. "What have you done?" and then the horrified cry as Doña Maria tried to stop him from taking the poison—"Answer me—speak to me! I pardon you and I love you, I believe you!"

"No, no, Mademoiselle." Victor Hugo had risen and come over to her side. "Not quite like that, if you please." His voice was courtly but firm. "Lean a little forward and stare for just a second. You cannot believe what has happened. Then cry, 'Answer me——'"

The director of the play held his breath. Sarah had learned through discipline and struggle to hold her temper in check, still it could burst out in fury now and then, as he only knew too well. It was unheard of for an author, even Victor Hugo, to offer advice on acting; unasked-for advice.

For a second Sarah was indignant. She had thought she was playing the scene quite well. And what did an author know about acting anyway? But this was Victor Hugo. Her indignation simmered down. She thought about what he had said, grudgingly admitted to herself that his advice could be right, tried it, and then smiled radiantly and graciously upon him.

"Monsieur Hugo, thank you; you were correct. The leaning forward—it was just what the scene needed."

From that moment on they were friends. He was a good deal older than she, yet he treated her with a grave, thoughtful respect that meant much to her. And once, when she did not deserve this respect and he treated her with something quite different, the rebuke was stinging.

It was on a day when the director was working with several other actors in a scene where Doña Maria had no part. Sarah was restless, moving about, not knowing or caring much whether she was disturbing the others. Finally she jumped onto a table and sat there, swinging her legs in her long skirts, her frivolous manner jarring with the serious tone of the play.

From his seat in the darkened auditorium came the quiet voice of Victor Hugo:

"A Queen of Spain, honest and respectable,
Should not sit thus upon a table."

He had made up the rhyme on the spur of the moment. Said
like that, in his quiet, gentle way, it was more punishment than
a long scolding from anyone else. The whole cast stopped and
looked at Sarah. Flushing, humiliated, but knowing she deserved
it, she got down quickly from the table and said to them all, "I am
sorry."

The understanding between Victor Hugo and Sarah Bernhardt was one between two artists. She could take criticism from
him because she knew he spoke only in the interests of the play,
never from a wish to hurt her; she knew, too, that he would not
bother to criticize her if he didn't think she had talent.

He told her, "I think, Mademoiselle, that you were born to be
an actress."

This was a surprising thought.

"Wouldn't it be odd if it were true and that it was my destiny
to be an actress, always?" she asked Madame Guerard that evening
as the two of them made ready to give a small party in her apartment. "I've always thought it was such an accident, really. I went
into the Conservatoire to escape a life I didn't like at home and
then, later, when I felt I couldn't marry Henri I remained an
actress because it was the only thing I knew to do. But *suppose*
it was *meant* to be—how different a viewpoint it becomes."

Madame was in the kitchen, anxiously watching the progress of
a chicken casserole while she peeled potatoes at the sink. She left
them both for a second and came to stand in the doorway to watch
Sarah, who was vigorously polishing the mirror over the bookcase.

"How so different?" Madame asked.

"Because when I agreed to go to the Conservatoire I thought I
was sacrificing myself: I wanted to be a nun. Then I thought it
was a tremendous sacrifice to give up Henri. Now I am not so
sure. Not that I didn't love him and still do—but I wonder if marriage, without the theater, would not have been intolerable after
a while?"

"I agree," the older woman said briskly. "You know I always

tell you your faults and scold you for your tempers, Sarah, but there's one thing that's very important: you are honest about yourself. Sooner or later you face up to facts."

"I wish I could face up to this furniture as easily." Sarah looked about her with distaste. The sofa had been reupholstered but in an inexpensive, plain material; a new and lovely writing table only emphasized how tasteless were the chairs and bookcase. "Oh, someday I'm going to burn the whole lot and buy only the best. I'm going to have a beautiful house and you shall come and live with me, and Maurice will go to the best schools and have a pony to ride and I'll have new dresses and eat hothouse grapes and——"

"And right now you'd better be thinking about this chicken casserole or there won't be a party tonight." Both women rushed into the kitchen and began hurrying the preparations for dinner. "Why you want to give a party tonight I can't imagine—the night of the opening of *Ruy Blas*. Who is invited?"

"Just François Coppée and George Sand and Paul Porel, an actor, and ourselves," Sarah said. "You know how badly I suffer from stage fright, so I thought if I planned this little early supper it would take my mind off the performance for a few hours. Then all of you can go together to the theater."

The supper was good, though simple. Sarah needn't have worried, either, about her furniture; her guests were not the kind who required fancy surroundings. They were all intellectuals, full of life and the excitement of living and making, each in his or her own way, their paths toward splendid careers. They were clever and witty and liked Sarah as much for her intelligence as for her talent.

Afterward they had a box at the Odéon for the opening performance of *Ruy Blas*. George Sands leaned forward and touched Madame Guerard's clenched hands as the house darkened, the gas lamps at the footlights flickered, and the curtain slowly rose. "Don't worry," she whispered. "It will be all right."

It was more than just all right. From the first moment it was a triumph and, most especially, Sarah's triumph. In her white lace gown touched with silver, a white lace mantilla over her beautiful hair, she was everything that Victor Hugo had imagined when he wrote of Doña Maria—a beautiful and gracious queen, a passionate and tragic queen, one who moved the audience to actual tears over her remorse at Ruy Blas' death.

The little party in the box had decided among themselves that they would clap so loudly that everyone else would follow their lead. Instead, they found themselves drowned out in the tumult of applause at the end of the play, their own "Bravo's!" lost in the wild cheering.

The next morning Sarah was still in bed, just waking up to receive seven-year-old Maurice's visit, when Madame Guerard arrived with the morning newspapers under her arm.

"Good morning, Madame. Good morning, Maurice," Sarah said sleepily. "Put that pillow over here, son, and you can sit next to me and have a second breakfast with me. I should be exhausted but I'm not. Let's see what the newspapers have to say about *Ruy Blas.*"

While the maid brought in breakfasts on trays, they searched through the pages. Madame Guerard found the important one.

"Listen. This is what Monsieur Sarcey says——"

"Sarcey. Francisque Sarcey? You have *Le Temps?* Oh, read it, please. That he should even mention it is something."

Madame held the paper up so that the morning light fell on the page and she could read more easily. "He says that you have received from nature the gift of wearied and melancholy dignity. Every motion you made was noble and harmonious; when you got up or sat down, whether you walked or half turned, the long folds of your gown laced with silver hung around you with a poetical grace——"

Sarah could stand it no longer. She held out her hand, begging for the paper. She wanted to read it herself.

Sarcey wrote:

> The voice is languishing and tender, her delivery so true in rhythm and so clear in utterance that never a syllable is lost, even when the words float from her lips like a caress. And how marvelously she follows the curve of a speech, letting it unfurl without a break, maintaining the harmony of its inflexible line. And with what delicate and telling intonations she underlines certain words, giving them an extraordinary value.

70

She lay back, her heart beating rapidly. Sarcey had at last acknowledged her. And with such praise! Not a line of criticism, not a caution or a sign that he had been disappointed in anything she had done, which was unusual for him. True, his review of *Ruy Blas* was a short one and he had devoted much more space to a review of a play he had seen two nights before at the Comédie Française, but he had truly liked her performance; that was the main thing.

Maurice, solemnly pretending to be a waiter, ran between the two women with sugar for their coffee and butter for their rolls, and now offered Sarah her napkin, which had fallen to the floor.

"Thank you, *garçon*," she said, falling in with his game. He smiled with delight. It was a smile that transformed his face from make-believe gravity into the gleeful one of a small boy.

"May I trouble the *garçon* to ask the chef if there are any more rolls in the kitchen?"

Instantly he became the waiter once more. He marched stiffly to the door, then bowed. "Certainly, Madame," he said, as he left. "At once, Madame." He poked his head around the corner once more to grin, then vanished.

I think he is truly a happy little boy, Sarah thought. A rather sober one sometimes, but a happy one. I can be proud of that.

She lay back on her pillow. She thought of last night: the stage fright that came as she waited to go on, the forgetfulness of it and everything else except Doña Maria as she walked out onto the stage, the exalted feeling of power that grew and grew as she knew she was creating Victor Hugo's heroine into a living, breathing, actual creature.

It came to her then that she loved acting. Suddenly she knew that she wouldn't want to be anyone else in the world but Sarah Bernhardt, actress. It had been a sacrifice to give up Henri and love, but it would have been a much more terrible sacrifice to have been forced to give up the theater.

Madame Guerard had found another long review in another paper.

"You must hear this one, Sarah. Theodore de Banville describes you like this:

"She is the only player whom the Creator has fashioned solely for the art of play-acting: tall as Rosalind, slender enough for any disguise, she is in so high a degree poetry incarnate that even when she is still and mute we are aware that her gait as well as her voice is subservient to a lyrical rhythm. . . . A great actress should be able to play Juliet and Lady Macbeth, Iphigenie and Eriphile . . ., consequently she must be neither dark nor fair. Thus Sarah Bernhardt, with her beautiful Dutch coloring, is neither fair nor dark. If she sprinkles her hair with water, it is fair; pomade turns it brown, and it is so naturally curled and waved . . . in so wondrous a shock . . . that she has only to ruffle it and plunge a pin into it to change it into the most elegant and complex of hairdresses. She has the face of a Nereid . . ."

The ringing doorbell interrupted the reading. It was a messenger with a sheaf of roses from Victor Hugo. A note of gratitude came next from Monsieur Duquesnal.

More bouquets came, and more notes. While Madame Guerard read them and arranged the flowers in bowls and vases, Sarah dressed so that she could take Maurice to the park. She was almost ready when her good friend brought in another note and handed it to her silently.

Sarah took it. "It is from Monsieur Perrin of the Comédie Française! He asks if it would be convenient for me to call upon him in his office this afternoon."

"I know. I read the note. Are you going?"

"Do you know what this means? He isn't asking me to come in to discuss the weather; he must want me to come back after my contract is through at the Odéon." Sarah was amazed.

"Are you going?" Madame repeated.

"To see him? Yes, of course. But would I return there? I don't know. The Comédie Française is still the great theater in Paris. I'm honored that they should want me back; it's most unusual after the way I left them. But these six years at the Odéon have been such happy ones. The managers have been good to me and the audiences seem like old friends. Still, would I ever be considered a first-rate actress in France if I weren't connected with the Comédie Française? . . . That's the difficulty."

She decided to take Maurice first to the park, then to Aunt

Rosine's which would leave her free to go on to the Comédie Française. Almost defiantly, before she left, she pinned on her coat a cheap little bouquet that had come that morning, wrapped in newspaper. But they were from five of her best "friends" in the audience—the students.

She wore them proudly.

Once again she walked through the side door of the Comédie Française, gave her name to the concièrge, waited until he pressed a button that released the lock of the door, entered, and turned to the left up the stairs. Once again she passed by the famous paintings and busts of the actors. Then she was in the hallway and being ushered into Monsieur Perrin's office.

He had replaced Manager Eduoard Thierry. He was new; he had no memories of a naughty girl who had been hurt and who had hurt others, who had broken her contract. He was all smiles and friendliness.

"I have followed your career these past few years with interest, Mademoiselle. You are to be congratulated on your Zanetto in *Le Passant* and now for your Doña Maria in *Ruy Blas*. We are prepared to offer you a contract at the Comèdie Française."

"As a *pensionnaire*?"

He sighed. "Unfortunately yes—just at first. But it will be a mere formality. An actress of your standing is not coming here on probation. It is necessary to make certain concessions to our rules that one must serve a little time before becoming a *sociétaire*. I can promise you a *sociétaire's* contract. Your salary will, of course, be that of a *sociétaire* from the very start. You will receive twelve thousand francs; more when the title is yours officially."

She was earning nine thousand franc's now.

"My contract at the Odéon still has a little time to run, Monsieur l'Directeur," she said.

"Oh, but we want you to come now! Just as soon as the performances of *Ruy Blas* are finished—naturally you cannot walk out on a play. But your acting in it has created quite a stir, and while the play is still on I can get around the objections which, you understand, some of the more conservative members of the company might make to your returning. However, if you wait, who

73

knows? You might be cast in an indifferent play next and your success in this be forgotten."

She left him, very much confused and torn in spirit. Legally her contract was still in force at the Odéon, actually she knew she had returned the managers a hundredfold anything they had given her or chanced on her. She owed them nothing. She simply liked them and did not want to hurt them.

Once inside the Comédie Française after such a long time, she knew it was important to her career to be a part of it. She had reached the point where a second-rank theater was holding her back. Only France's first theater could place her in a position where she could receive the attention she felt she deserved.

Perplexed, she kept the meeting with Perrin to herself for a week before she told the two managers, Duquesnal and de Chilly.

De Chilly was, unfortunately, not well and in a bad mood. No sooner had she begun to speak than he was incensed and suspicious. "Nonsense! I happen to know that the *sociétaires* would never let you come back there. I was told so by one of them. You are just making up the whole story so that you can force us to raise your salary."

Sarah may have subdued her temper but she had not lost it. "Do you want me to prove I'm telling you the truth?" she demanded angrily.

"You can't prove it. I know better."

She left the office without another word, walked to the Comédie Française, and signed the contract. She was so furious that the pen trembled in her hand.

{ *8* }

It was done! Sarah Bernhardt was once again a member of the Comédie Française.

But with such a difference! Though still a *pensionnaire,* she had her own large dressing room and she was considered, by most of the company, on a level with the *sociétaires* . . .

It was Marie Lloyd who put it into words. She was unchanged. The beautiful, sweet young girl had became a beautiful, sweet woman with as much affection for Sarah as ever. She threw her arms around her friend as the two met backstage.

"I heard you had come!" she exclaimed with excitement. "I am so glad."

Sarah's eyes filled with tears. Marie had tried to be friends after she had left the company, and it was Sarah's fault that their friendship had been broken off. "I'm glad too, Marie. Do you remember when we first came here like two schoolgirls, so awed and so scared?"

"And Monsieur Davenne told us about Molière and all the great names who had acted here? And we walked out on the stage? My knees were shaking."

Just then a large, stout woman passed them without speaking, looking very pointedly the other way.

"Wasn't that Madame Nathalie?" asked Sarah.

"Yes. Don't mind her. She and a few of the others—well, you know how it is. They're stiff-necked and jealous. They resent your coming back like this."

"Through the back door, so to speak?" said Sarah. A little of the pleasure of the day had begun to fade. She felt herself stiffening, tensing for the next rebuff. A large salary was not going to compensate for these hurts.

"Well, after all, she can't forget that you slapped her—though I think you were perfectly justified," Marie consoled her.

Sarah stared at her friend. It had been so long ago. Did people hang on so long to old resentments? She had forgotten what it was like at the Comédie Française and how huge little things could seem to people whose lives had followed a less eventful course than hers.

The two young women walked on slowly toward Marie's dressing room. Everywhere Sarah looked there were memories coming back to delight or sadden her: here in these wings she had waited on the night of her debut, a scared youngster; there, just above those steps, she had slapped Madame Nathalie; here was the wig-maker coming toward her, acompanied as usual by his son who was learning how to make wigs, as was the tradition in his family.

They passed an extremely pretty woman who walked with a light tripping step and who smiled brightly at both of them. Marie informed Sarah that she was Mademoiselle Sophie Croizette, the current reigning actress—if the Comédie Française could be said to have such—just now. "She's especially good in coquette parts where she can be pert and charming. She has a large following. I think you'll like her—she's very nice."

They were almost at the door of Marie's dressing room when a voice halted them, calling:

"Mademoiselle Bernhardt? It is Sarah Bernhardt, isn't it?"

She turned in surprise. The voice was unfamiliar and the young man who was hurrying toward her, hand outstretched, was a stranger to her. Surely if she had seen this tall, handsome young man before she would have remembered him? How could she forget anyone with such striking good looks?

Then she remembered. "Mounet Sully! Jean Mounet Sully, of course. You played with me at the Odéon a few years ago." But Sarah was thinking to herself how incredible it was that a man could have changed so much. At the Odéon he had been an insignificant player; if he had been as handsome then as now it must have been concealed by an unhappy mood or a lack of confidence in himself.

Certainly this was not the case now. He was smiling; he carried himself with an air of supreme happiness with himself and the world—and with her. "Yes, I'm Mounet. I heard you were coming and have been waiting to greet you. It seems to me that we have something in common, we two. We have both been hired and they're all waiting to see what we are going to do with ourselves. And I suspect that there are some who are hoping we'll fail. But we won't. We may be outcasts but we'll show them, won't we?"

There was something so openly, naïvely blunt about this young man's way of putting things, something so tolerant in his arrogance —as if he were so sure of himself that he could afford to laugh off anyone's feelings about him—that Sarah didn't even mind his calling her an "outcast." In fact, she liked the idea of their having a bond between them.

"So we should help each other?" Tall as she was, she had to put her head back to look up at him.

He nodded his blond curls. "We should. You are considered unpredictable and I'm called crazy, but we both know we can act."

Marie, waiting and watching, felt something magnetic between these two.

"But why are you called crazy?" Sarah asked.

"Because for such a long time I couldn't act and everyone told me I couldn't act, but I kept hanging on. I knew I could. I knew it was just a question of time and work. Then, suddenly—just like that—I jumped from being terrible to being very good. But I have to do things my own way; that's why they say I'm crazy."

"Then we are both mad in the same way." She gave him her hand to say good-by, but he held it tightly in a fervent clasp.

"Promise to come tonight and sit out front and watch me," he begged.

She promised and then followed Marie and settled down for a long chat.

That night she saw, with astonishment, that this Mounet Sully was no longer the mediocre player he had been at the Odéon. Now he was acting exceptionally well—as if, as he said, his talents had been buried before and were just now coming out into the light.

She sought out Monsieur Perrin the next day. "Well, Monsieur le Directeur, what have you in mind for me?"

"Why, nothing at all at the moment, Mademoiselle. You have only just come. The schedule is quite full at present. So you may have a little rest, which I'm sure you will enjoy after playing and rehearsing so constantly as you were at the Odéon."

She started to protest, then stopped. Of course. The system of the Comédie Française. The huge company. What else had she expected? All must wait their turn.

But what am I to do with myself? she wondered. Maurice is seven and in school. He doesn't need me all day. My friends are busy working. I have so little in common with Mama and Aunt Rosine I don't enjoy visiting them.

The next few weeks were difficult for her. It was like the sudden stopping of a high-powered machine. The idleness left her spinning without forward motion, without any traction.

She could not help being a little envious of Mademoiselle Croizette. Currently in a play that was doing very well, she was praised by the critics and loved by the public. In spite of herself, Sarah listened to the gossip backstage that Monsieur Perrin favored Croizette because she was bringing in large sums of money at the box office.

Fixing up her dressing room took up some of Sarah's time, though it left her in the queer apathy that idleness always produced in her. It was good tactics to spend money on her dressing room because doing so let the whole company know she considered herself in fact a *sociétaire*.

She even went into debt for the ivory and gold chairs, the new ivory mantelpiece, the jade figures on it, the green watered-silk hangings, and the brilliantly flowered couch. But it hurt her to see the contrast between that room and the shabbiness at home.

Perrin finally gave her a role in Alexandre Dumas' *The Girl of Belle Isle* but it was not a good part for her. She did not work hard enough beforehand; she worked too hard on stage to make up for it.

The Girl of Belle Isle was a complete failure for her.
Sarcey wrote:

> . . . It was a disappointment when she came onstage. Whether her powdered hair did not suit her face, or whether she was terribly pale from stage fright, it was not a very agreeable impression to see emerging from a long black hood this long white face, from which the sparkle of the eyes had disappeared and in which only the gleaming teeth stood out . . .

Sarah read the notice in her dressing room. She threw the paper across the room, snatched up a vase of flowers and flung it after the paper. The flowers scattered over the floor, the water soaked into the carpet, the vase splintered into fragments. She paid no attention.

To have a failure like this, *just now*, at such a critical time! She paced up and down. It was Perrin's fault. It was the director's fault. It was the costume-maker's . . .

Then she stopped raging and began to face facts: it was no one's fault but my own, actually. What difference if Perrin favors someone else and gives me poor parts? I'm responsible for my acting. I neither studied nor worked nor rehearsed properly. The costume-maker would have made something better for me if I had cared enough to suggest anything. I know what I can wear and she doesn't.

Sarah realized then that somehow, she would have to adjust herself to the system of the Comédie Française, not fight it. She would have to find some way of keeping her energy always at its highest peak.

The next role for her was as Junie in Racine's *Britannicus* and— wonderful news! Mounet Sully was to play opposite her as Nero. True to the pact they had pledged each other that first day, they worked together outside of the theater, at her home. They rehearsed the scenes they had together; they criticized each other freely and honestly; they incited and stirred each other to attempt more and more subtle intonations of their two characters.

The night of *Britannicus* startled Perrin and the audience. It was not only that Sarah and Mounet Sully played Junie and Nero exceptionally well. What startled everyone was the spark of electricity, the leap of excitement almost physically visible each time Sarah and Mounet were in the same scene.

Why, thought Marie, watching from the wings, those two are in love!

The whole of the Comédie Française were soon convinced that the two were in love. Sarah was beautiful, Mounet Sully was incredibly handsome. When the two of them walked down the halls together or stood talking and laughing, they were a striking couple. That which drew a circle around them and separated them from other people was their vitality, their vibrant sense of life, which was heightened when they were together.

Everywhere they went they were surrounded by an aura of romance. Their fellow workers looked on them fondly, with the

79

sentiment everyone feels for those in love. When they strolled down Paris streets together people turned to stare at them. If they went to their favorite café, the head waiter always took them to a special table which his romantic soul had marked out as theirs.

Both Sarah and Mounet were beginning to be publicly known. Sooner or later, in café or street, someone would recognize them—"Sarah Bernhardt and Mounet Sully!"—the whispers began. And, since all the world enjoys a love story, especially such a one as this with a fairy-tale prince and princess in it, everyone beamed and smiled on them.

Sarah was confused. For the first time since Henri de Ligne, she felt that her heart had been touched. A golden, misty haze of romance had enveloped herself and Mounet; it quickened her spirit and made her feel young and gay. When her mind would whisper doubts, she did not want to listen.

It was much too exciting to have Mounet waiting for her after a rehearsal with a hired carriage, to go riding with him under the chestnut trees, to have him hold her hand while they talked, endlessly, of the theater. Always the theater. Always of their plans, their ideas, their work.

It was Mounet who brought her the wonderful news.

"Sarah! You're playing *Andromaque*! Perrin just told me." He grabbed her and waltzed her round and round her dressing room. "This is your chance, Sarah darling."

Waltzing, she was as ecstatic with the news as he was. She picked up a corner of her long skirts with one hand and swayed to an imaginary music neither of them needed. "Andromaque—Andromaque—I'm to be Andromaque—at last, at last. Oh, stop, Mounet! I'm out of breath. I have to stop and think about it."

Leaning back in her chair and looking up at him, she sobered. "It's wonderful, but it's also frightening. *Andromaque*, *Phèdre*, *Athalie*—any actress who takes the title role in any three of those Racine plays is stepping into dangerous territory, you know. Only an actress with true dramatic ability can play them."

He shrugged. "That's true. But what are *you* frightened of?"

She drove herself to work and study. There were few rides in the park now. Nothing, not even Mounet, must take a single moment she could give to the mastery of this part.

Opening night she stood in the wings, shivering with stage fright as usual. Mounet came to stand beside her. He pulled aside a fold in the curtain so they could peek out at the audience.

"Look—there's Francisque Sarcey." Mounet pointed out the small, round figure with the bald head and the short, bristly beard. Sarcey squeezed his fat stomach past an elderly dowager into his favorite seat. His sharp eyes gave one glance at the audience, then fixed themselves on the printed program.

Sarah shivered again.

"Darling, don't be afraid. Why, your lips are blue. What have you to be afraid of?" Almost without nerves himself, Mounet looked at her with consternation. "You know your part backward and forward."

"So does everyone else in Paris. That's the trouble. If I were to make a mistake in a single line, anyone in the audience could correct me. That's not it." Her ice-cold hands sought his for comfort. "To play Andromaque one must have something else. I have thought about it: why should Andromaque, a widow with a child, a captive, still in love with her dead husband—why should she so attract Pyrrhus that he would be willing to sacrifice everything for her? I've watched other actresses and nothing about them convinced me that she had any special charm. Just a good-looking woman. Yet she must have had a most potent charm."

There was no time for Mounet to answer. Already the lights were dimming. From behind the curtain came the six loud knocks that always preceded the opening of a play at the Comédie Française. Other theaters used the traditional three—one for the king, one for the court, one for the gentlefolk surrounding the court. Only the Comédie Française used six and the reason was lost in antiquity.

Slowly the curtain went up to reveal the Grecian courtyard of a king's palace, with its stately white columns and the curved steps in tiers below, down to the flat space at the front of the stage.

Mounet gave her hand a last squeeze before he, as Orestes, in long Greek toga, walked out onto the stage with the actor who played his friend, Pylades.

Sarah could hear the abrupt hush in the audience. Then the clear but worried voices of the two men as they spoke of Orestes' voyage from Greece to this court of King Pyrrhus. Pyrrhus was pledged to marry Hermione, whom Orestes loved, but rumors had reached his ears that the King was enamoured of the captive Andromaque.

What, asked Pylades, was Orestes' mission to this court?

He was to persuade Pyrrhus to kill Andromaque's little son! People feared that this child of Hector might someday take revenge upon all of Greece for the noble Hector's death. As long as the boy lived he was a menace.

As Sarah stood listening, another actor in the costume of a Grecian warrior came to stand in the wings. This was Pyrrhus, awaiting his cue. She was hardly conscious of him, barely listening to the voices on stage. Her nerves were reaching the pitch she feared and yet knew would come, tensing her, sharpening every nerve and brain cell, stirring all her emotions to the fullest.

Pyrrhus strode out on the stage to greet Orestes haughtily and listen with arrogant refusal to his demand that he kill the boy. After Orestes exited, Pyrrhus confided to his friends that he hoped Orestes and Hermione found themselves to be in love again. He loved Andromaque.

A hand touched Sarah's arm. It was the actress who played her confidante, Cephissa. It was time.

In the few steps it took for her to go from the darkened wings to the brightly lighted stage, a transformation took place. Sarah Bernhardt was left behind to wait in the shadows; Andromaque, a captive Greek widowed queen, took her place.

When Andromaque appeared before the audience a gasp of astonishment went up all over the theater. Traditionally, all actresses who played the roles of Grecian women did so in long gowns of white. This Andromaque was in black, with a long flowing veil—also of black.

Whispers spread through the theater. "In black! But why not? After all, Andromaque is a widow——"

82

Then Pyrrhus was speaking, asking in tones unlike his usual warrior's arrogance if it was he whom she was seeking.

Andromaque replied that she was seeking her son, the only being left to her. Pyrrhus, disappointed and angry, threatened her with Orestes' demand. If she would consent to marry him, Pyrrhus, her son would be spared. If she refused, her son would die. Andromaque replied to his ultimatum with scorn.

As she spoke, Sarcey leaned forward. So did others in the audience. The critic was puzzled by a nuance, a difference between this Andromaque and any other. What was this quality in her voice and in each gesture that was so strange a mixture of invitation and rejection? Andromaque was saying no; she meant no. But everything about the woman—her movements and her personality —was so alluring that Pyrrhus or any man would be madly in love with her.

Sarcey listened and watched more intently. This Bernhardt was injecting a quality into the character he had never heard or seen before.

Suddenly he realized what it was—a strong emanation of feminine seductiveness, unconscious on the part of Andromaque. As natural to her as breathing and with no intent to charm the man she hated. It was just there. For the first time Sarcey felt that Andromaque was utterly convincing as a captive who would turn a king's head so that he would lose all sense of honor and duty.

Whatever Bernhardt's doing, it's genius, Sarcey thought, and hastily scribbled a note for himself in the darkness.

He did not know it, but Sarah herself was unaware of what she was doing. But all of the intelligence she had brought to bear in her role, all of the craft, all of the emotion, the probing into Andromaque's character, her special worry on just this particular thing, had fused together. Out of it her special creative genius had solved the question. An element had been lacking. Now it was here.

The audience felt it and was stirred. They felt this seductive charm reaching out to them, arousing them to the point where they could sympathize with Pyrrhus and at the same time believe that Andromaque truly wanted only peace and her son.

The curtain came down. When it rose again Hermione and Orestes were onstage. Sarcey barely listened, though his trained eye was noting the excellence of Mounet Sully's acting. The critic was still wondering how Sarah Bernhardt could have achieved the subtlety in Andromaque's character. He had seen many actresses play the queen as haughty and outraged, as womanly and motherly. She was all these things, but she had to be more than that. As Bernhardt portrayed her—that, thought Sarcey, makes Andromaque unique, believable, and real.

Andromaque appeared again; this time to plead with Hermione to intercede for her and her son. In the face of Hermione's refusal and Pyrrhus' decision to kill the boy, Andromaque finally consented to the marriage. Then came her immortal lines as she told her confidant that once the marriage was performed it would be her duty and her right to kill herself and rejoin her dead husband:

> ". . . since a victim's needed,
> I'll promise Pyrrhus all that's left of life,
> And I will bind him to my boy with words
> Unspeakable and sacred. After that,
> This hand shall, straightway, with a fatal blow
> Cut through the cord of life that's true no longer,
> And so I'll keep me free from stain."

The haughty voice changed almost immediately to a mother's yearning:

> "Recount, each day, his father's virtues to him,
> And whisper, sometimes, of a mother's love."

Sarcey, who had sat through hundreds of such performances dry-eyed, was but dimly aware of the tears that misted his eyes. All around him women were sobbing and men were trying to conceal their emotional response to the tragedy being so movingly enacted on the stage.

The end was near at hand. The marriage of Andromaque and Pyrrhus took place, followed by the murder of Pyrrhus by Orestes. Andromaque remained queen, once again a widow.

It was over. The curtain fell.

Onstage, Sarah and the rest of the cast listened. There was utter silence—not a sound from the audience. The players looked at each other, alarmed and astonished. Where was the applause?

It came with the suddenness of a thunderclap, as if emotions had been held in, tightly reined, and had suddenly given way with the impact of an explosion. It was deafening, wild, breaking the bounds of polite behavior.

When the curtain went up to reveal the cast standing there, the volume of applause grew louder if that was possible. There were handclaps and "Bravo's!" from down below; there were yelling and screaming from the top boxes where the students were.

"Andromaque—Andromaque—Sarah Bernhardt—" they yelled.

Mounet pushed Sarah forward. People were standing, but there was no movement toward the aisles or to the exits. They had risen to pay homage to Sarah's performance. Down came the curtain and up again for another bow from the cast. Up and down, up and down, yet the audience was in no mood to leave, nor did the applause diminish. It was an ovation for a spectacular performance —a once-in-a-lifetime performance—and this is what the audience was saying to each other, now they had found breath for words.

"We shall not see another *Andromaque* like that one!"

"That is something to tell our grandchildren, isn't it? That we saw one of the greatest *Andromaques* ever given on a stage."

But as the audience finally made its way out into the lobby there were a few veteran theatergoers who were cautious.

"Oh, I grant you that Sarah Bernhardt was great tonight. I shall never forget such a voice, one that thrilled me as never before, such an Andromaque who was truly a woman who could topple thrones—but she has found her level in this. As a tragic actress of such parts she will do very well in the future, but I doubt very much if she can play other things as well."

"She can play anything!" A student rudely broke into the conversation. "You did not see her as Zanetto in *Le Passant*."

"Here, here! I wasn't speaking to you——"

"But I'm speaking to you and I say Sarah Bernhardt is the finest actress in all of France today."

Arguments broke out with fierce partisanship. The students, feeling Sarah's triumph as if it were their own, went cheerfully and vigorously looking for trouble.

Backstage, Mounet and Sarah and Marie staged their own victory celebration in Sarah's dressing room.

"You really should rest, Sarah," Marie cautioned her. "Your face is so white and your eyes are burning."

"I know but I don't feel tired. I feel like staying up all night. I'm starving." Sarah helped herself to the tray piled high with sandwiches and fruit.

Mounet was eating hungrily too. "You did it, Sarah. You showed them. You were wonderful. I was too"—complacently, and laughing at himself—"but nothing to compare with you."

"Very well to say all this, Mounet, but what next? Do you suppose Perrin will have learned anything? Or will he go on scheduling plays that Croizette can do best and leave nothing but crumbs for the rest of us?"

He protested vigorously. "How can you say that after tonight? You're being unfair to Perrin. He does his best. He has to satisfy a whole company and keep us all playing as often as possible."

"Tonight was Racine." Sarah licked a few crumbs off her fingers. "The Comédie Française always plays Racine. I'm speaking of *new* plays."

"Well, you can't blame him for playing safe and getting new plays that feature Croizette, since she already has a following. He'd be taking a big chance with us."

They were still arguing about it when he left her at her front door. It struck her then, for the first time, that she and Mounet always talked of the theater, nothing else.

Four days later she played the small part of Aricie in *Phèdre* for a matinee. This time she and Mounet played opposite each other as young lovers doomed to tragedy; this time Sarcey capitulated entirely to Sarah and wrote of her wonderful voice, her grace, and her capacity for strong emotion.

The danger was there, however, that she was being "typed" as a Racine actress only.

She argued with Perrin. "If you'd just give me a chance to prove myself in a new and different kind of a play. That's all I ask—a chance."

"Very well." He had had so much of her arguments he was tired of them. "Very well." He took a thick manuscript from a drawer in his desk and handed it to her. "Here is a new drama the committee has chosen. But I warn you, yours will be a secondary role. Mademoiselle Croizette has the principal character in it. You will play Berthe de Savigny. Read it and tell me if you are willing."

His secretary reminded him he was expected backstage, whereupon he excused himself and left. Sarah settled down to read *Le Sphinx*.

When Monsieur Perrin returned in half an hour she was still there.

She greeted him, smiling. "I shall be happy to play the part of Berthe de Savigny, Monsieur le Directeur," she said demurely.

Having expected a flat refusal, more arguments, fireworks, perhaps, he was taken aback. "Fine, fine," he muttered. He showed her out, still wondering why she wanted the smaller part where she would be put in the shadow of Croizette.

When the play opened he found out. He realized what Sarah had guessed from her first reading: Croizette was not capable of projecting the emotions demanded of her in the last act, where she must take poison. Sarah was able, with her smaller part, to completely outplay and outshine the other.

Watching that last act from his reserved box, Perrin put his head in his hands and groaned.

The next day Sarcey wrote:

Mademoiselle Croizette drank a bottle of poison and fell dying in a chair. Then we witnessed a really hideous spectacle. With the aid of certain tricks . . . the actress' face suddenly became greenish, horribly decomposed, wrinkling in fearful contractions . . . her head was shaken in the convulsions of lockjaw. In the part of Berthe de Savigny, which ceased to be a minor one, Mademoiselle Sarah Bernhardt won the applause of the connoisseurs. She played with noble and discreet grace . . . she knew how to evoke applause with a few words or a gesture of her outstretched hand.

"Poor Croizette," Marie said. "She can't play tragedy so she tried to use all kinds of tricks—green paint on her face and stuff like that—to make her dying look real. Sarah, I think you knew she couldn't play it and that's why you wanted to do Berthe de Savigny."

Sarah laughed. "I wanted to act Berthe because I knew I could. Sophie isn't upset about it. She says it's taught her a lesson not to try tragedy again."

But with her success in Le Sphinx came a great change. Now it was no longer a question of who was the best actress at the Comédie Française or in all of France. Nor was there any doubt that Sarah Bernhardt was capable of more than one kind of role. At the top of her profession, with the acknowledged supremacy that no one at the theater could doubt, it was decided to entrust her now with the part that few actresses dared to try since the famous Rachel had made it so much her own in the years past.

She was to play Phèdre.

This most difficult of Racine's characters was to be her test. The role in Phèdre is the role of a woman tortured almost to insanity by the love she has in secret for her own stepson. Again the scene was ancient Greece.

Madame Guerard, who by now had given up her own apartment and come to live with Sarah, waited after rehearsals with special dishes to tempt her appetite. Little Maurice felt Madame's tension and tried in his boyish way to help. Mounet worried; Marie Lloyd fluttered around her solicitously.

Only Sarah was serene. It was as if all her work and experience had been leading up to this culmination. Phèdre was her role; she knew it.

From the moment when, on the night of December 21, 1874, she walked on the stage as Phèdre, trembling and half dead with the torment of her guilty love to the moment when she learns that her stepson Hippolyte not only despises her but cares for Aricie, Sarah Bernhardt swept the audience with her into the throes of almost inhuman agony and passion.

Her performance was a stupendous moment in theatrical history and the audience knew it. When it was over they refused to let her go until she had come back over and over again to receive their applause. They cried their bravos through voices that were still raw with weeping; they saw her through eyes still wet with tears.

Early next morning the doorbell began ringing. The pounding of the knocker was incessant.

"You were wonderful, Sarah darling . . ." the note read from Mounet.

"Mademoiselle Bernhardt, I am a stranger to you but I must write to say I have never seen such a Phèdre——"

From Duquesnal: "I forgive you for deserting us, Sarah, after watching you last night."

"I had resigned myself, Mademoiselle Bernhardt, to never seeing another Phèdre as fine as Rachel's. I would not insult either of you by comparison. You are nothing alike. I can only say that I am a happy man that in my lifetime I have seen two such Phèdres." This was from a signature unknown to her.

"Divine, beautiful Sarah," the notes from the students called her.

With all the excitement and the interruptions it was noon before she had dressed and eaten her breakfast. Then it was time for Maurice to come home from school and, since he was not yet old enough to go to the theater, she had to tell him all about it.

"Tell me again, Mama, how many times did they applaud you?"

"Oh, hundreds!" she said gaily. "I was so excited I couldn't remember. It was all a dream, once it was over."

They were interrupted by the entrance of Mounet bringing flowers and a whole stack of newspapers. They read a few of the reviews together, then it was time for Sarah to bundle Maurice up warmly against the winter cold and send him off again to school.

When he was gone and Madame Guerard had taken her shopping basket to find vegetables for dinner, Mounet lingered. Suddenly and impetuously he said, "Sarah, why don't we marry?"

Just as suddenly Sarah knew she could not. All the illusion of being really in love with him disappeared.

"No, Mounet. I love you, but not in the way you must be to marry someone. We have a great affection for each other and a great bond, but it has solely and entirely to do with our being in the theater."

"I don't understand."

"Everyone thought we were in love. Everyone told us so; we grew to believe it. But what do we share? The same driving force to become the finest of actors. That's all. Marriage isn't a storybook romance. We would have to love each other and share all kinds of problems. I would have to see you when you aren't so handsome, with a cold in your head. You would have to see me frantic about money, worrying about Maurice—why, do you know, Mounet, Maurice hardly exists for you? I don't mean that you're unkind to him. You just don't think of him."

He was honest enough to know she was right, though it hurt. He loved her more than she thought. But he was single-minded in purpose and in spirit. The theater consumed him and his love for Sarah was part of his love for the theater.

"This won't make any difference, will it? We will still see each other and work together?" he asked.

She assured him that she wanted the closeness between them as much as he did. When he left, she was sad for a while. It was seldom that she felt lonely. She did now.

Then she straightened her shoulders. What next? I must go see Monsieur Perrin immediately and find out what the next production will be.

Again she had forgotten the "system" of the Comédie Française.

There was to be no next, not for a while, not right at this moment. It would take time, Perrin assured her. After all, there were other actors and a schedule already made up. Surely she would be glad of a little rest? There were some small parts coming up;

she was cast in them—she could have any of them she wanted. Monsieur Perrin was as patient as his taxing job and all his responsibilities permitted him to be.

"I don't object to playing small parts if only there were enough of them," she replied. "But what am I going to do with myself? I can't just sit and twiddle my thumbs."

"I don't know, Mademoiselle," he said helplessly. Why couldn't she be as easily satisfied as the others?

Sarah bought a piano and revived her practicing until she was able to play extremely well. She gave more parties, meeting more and more interesting people. She went more often to see her mother who was not well and had given up her own gay life for a sickbed.

Still, there were hours with nothing to do. The pent-up energy was making her restless and irritable again, she was beginning to take a positive and quite unwarrented dislike to Perrin.

Finally Georges Clairin, a very good painter and a new friend, suggested that she try her hand at painting. "Why not? I think you have a good eye for color and design."

She tried. Her paintings were poor, but she had enjoyed doing them. She changed to sculpture and found she had a small but real talent for it. The only difficulty was that she had to rent a studio; it was a nuisance going from home to studio, to theater, and back again.

Suddenly, one day, the most unexpected thing happened. Sarah was opening her mail that morning when she came upon one from a firm of lawyers quite unknown to her. She opened it, read it, and then ran into the living room, calling frantically for Madame Guerard.

"Look! I've inherited money—one hundred thousand francs from an aunt in Holland. I vaguely remember Mama speaking of her, but I don't think I ever met her. One hundred thousand francs! Think what that means—Oh, get your hat and coat, let's get dressed! We're going on the biggest shopping spree you ever saw. I'm going to buy a house and the most beautiful furniture ever made and a carriage, and Maurice can go to a good school. Come!"

"Sarah," protested Madame with a quiet smile, "you surely are not going out into the street like that? You have your coat and hat on and your gloves, but you're still wearing your bedroom slippers."

Because she could not find a house that had a studio, Sarah bought a lot at the corner of the Avenue de Villiers and the Rue Fortuny and built one to her own taste. It was a lavish taste; all the years of shabbiness and privation she made up for now in the most expensive way. Her studio was small, but it was part of the house and she could work there whenever she had free time.

It was in the studio that Marie Lloyd found her one rainy spring afternoon. Sarah was modeling the figures of a Breton peasant woman holding on her knees the body of her son.

"What are you going to call it?" Marie asked. She was puzzled at Sarah's interest in this strange hobby.

" 'After the Storm,' " Sarah said. She moved around to the other side to work on the head of the woman. As she did so her smock fell open.

Marie gasped. "You're wearing trousers!"

"Yes. Why not? I found skirts impossible in the studio; they got in my way and I was constantly tripping over them, or else they picked up every scrap of wet clay I dropped on the floor."

She saw Marie's round, astonished eyes and knew that by the next day another story would be added to the list of eccentricities of Sarah Bernhardt. Mademoiselle Bernhardt not only wore clothes on the street that were different from others—her long sheath dresses and high, flaring collars had become well known—now it would be said she wore pants like a man.

There was always gossip about her, which she ignored. Her romance with Mounet, her tantrums and tempers, her friendships with the intellectuals of Paris, her sculpture—all were exaggerated into wild stories.

"I came over today because I wanted to be the first to tell you that the *sociétaires* voted to take you in. You're a *sociétaire* now. Isn't that splendid?" Marie settled herself on a high stool to watch Sarah work.

"I doubt if it will change things for me, except to give me more

92

money. Thank goodness for that. I've about used up all of the hundred thousand francs . . ."

"Sarah! You haven't."

"Oh yes I have. For once I wanted all the things I could never afford. After patching and mending those chairs and that sofa for so many years, I wanted nothing about me that wasn't the best. Come and see." She wiped her hands on a piece of cotton cloth and led Marie on a tour of the completed house.

It was more than beautiful, it was magnificent. Marie was dazzled by the great crystal chandeliers in the drawing room, the rose brocade walls and the ivory satin curtains richly framing the tall windows that opened onto the stone balconies. Sarah's own suite of rooms, bedroom and study, were in green, exquisitely furnished, deceptively simple, with a portrait of her by Clairin dominating the green walls. Next door to hers, Maurice's rooms were everything that a boy could possibly wish for or imagine. Madame Guerard also had her own entire suite.

"And the dining salon!" Marie gasped. "Such silver and lovely Venetian glass! I think you could seat the whole company of the Comédie Française at that table"—with an envious glance down the length of the satin-polished surface.

"Not at the same time, I hope. Can't you imagine the hair-pulling and the squabbles that would break out?"

Marie said, "Oh, I know there are a lot of petty jealousies and gossip, but on the whole I think you also find much kindness and goodness and dignity backstage too."

"Of course, that's true. Did you know that Madame Nathalie is having her farewell performance? And that the first person she asked to be on the bill with her was me? I was sincerely touched. But it is a close-knit circle. Sometimes I can't breathe in it. Everyone is so smug and satisfied with being a *sociétaire*."

Marie was sweet and gentle, but she did not lack courage. "You are very wrong to complain. The system is a wonderful one. We have security, which means we can spend our efforts developing ourselves instead of running around frantically looking for work. Because we may have a big part one week and a small one the next, we don't star one person year after year at the expense of the others. Everyone is important but no one is too important. And because we must play all kinds of roles, it keeps us from becoming one-sided."

The system of the Comédie Française was, indeed, a most admirable one; almost perfect. It developed richly and fully the talents of the many. It was not the fault of the theater that Sarah was too much of an individual to fit in and that her talents had that streak of genius which could not be subordinated to other people's rules.

A maid entered. "Mademoiselle Bernhardt, there has been a message from your mother. She is seriously ill."

Sarah tore off the smock and rushed toward her bedroom. "Excuse me, Marie, but I must go immediately."

For months Julie lingered, dying. Sarah was in a play called *L'Étrangère*, by Alexandre Dumas, *fils*, and it was a severe task on her strength to run from the performance to her mother's bedside every day. Toward the end of April, Sarah moved into the apartment and never left her mother's side except for the few hours of each night's performance, until Julie died early in May of 1876.

Sarah collapsed and Marie took her place in *L'Étrangère*. Sarah was as grief-stricken as if her mother had been the fond, loving parent the daughter had always wanted her to be.

So popular had Sarah become with the Parisian public that they took this unusual absence of hers very much to heart. The newspapers had to print every day a special *Bulletin on the Health of Sarah Bernhardt* to reassure people that she was all right.

When she came back to work there was an unusual challenge for her. On November 27, Monsieur Perrin called together a group of *sociétaires* who would be the future cast for a new play called *Rome Vaincue* by Alexandre Parodi. As they sat around the table in the charming upstairs "green room" next to his office, he handed each of them the script and proceeded to tell them the story of Opimia, the Vestal Virgin of ancient Rome who had broken her vow of eternal chastity. For this crime she was to suffer the prescribed punishment: to be sewn alive in a sack, driven late at night so that no Roman could look upon her, to a place outside the city and there be buried alive.

Opimia was given one last chance to say good-by to her grandmother. When the two were alone she begged the old woman to stab her rather than let her suffer such a horrible and prolonged death. The old woman finally agreed and murdered her own grandchild. With this scene the play ended.

"The part of Opimia," Perrin announced, "will be taken by Mademoiselle Bernhardt."

He was about to go on and designate the rest of the roles when Sarah interrupted:

"Monsieur, would it be possible to make a change? May I ask a favor?"

"Perhaps," he answered cautiously.

"I should like to play the part of the grandmother instead."

They all looked at her, astonished. Almost as much as for her acting she had gained a reputation for her beauty. Opimia would be garbed in the lovely white robes of the Vestal Virgin; it would be a part to inspire pity and sympathy in an audience. She would look lovely and die gracefully. But to play an old crone of a grandmother . . . ?

Perrin objected. She argued. He pleaded. She was obstinate; she wanted that part. Finally he gave in.

If Perrin and the *sociétaires* were surprised, it was nothing to the shock of the audience when the curtain went up on the first night of the performance.

It was horrible to see this wrinkled, bent, black-clad, black-cloaked, shuffling old woman, blind and pathetic, instead of the much-talked-about beautiful Sarah Bernhardt.

But when the scene unfolded and they saw this blind old woman rise to the moment when she was torn between her love for her grandchild and the piteous knowledge that unless she killed this girl, she would suffer the worst possible lingering death; when her old back straightened and she extended her arms to heaven to beg the gods to release her from this decision; when she lowered them in resignation, groped her feeble, sightless way to where her granddaughter lay bound to her bed, then the audience understood that this play belonged to the grandmother and not to the pretty Opimia.

When the old hands shook, when tears streamed down the wrinkled cheeks as she fumbled in her own darkness to find the heart where her dagger must go; when at the fatal moment she shook off her years and became strong and sure just long enough to drive in the blade—then the audience knew why Sarah wanted that part.

Only a great actress could have done it. It was Sarah's claim to being such an actress, who needed no beautiful face or red-gold hair to bring tears and a sense of noble tragedy to her audience's heart.

After *Rome Vaincue* came a succession of little parts, then a revival of Victor Hugo's *Hernani*. The day after her performance in the leading role, Victor Hugo sent Sarah a note and a little package. The note read:

> Madame:
> You were great and you were charming. You moved even me, an old warrior, and at a certain moment, while the touched and delighted public was applauding you, I wept. That tear which you caused to flow is yours. Allow me to present it to you.
> Victor Hugo

The "tear" was a diamond in the shape of a tear drop, hung on a thin golden chain.

Overcome by the meaning and the beauty of such a gift, Sarah brought it to the theater that evening and showed it to Mounet Sully.

"Isn't it exquisite? I shall treasure it always. I feel that after this there could be no other achievement in life that I could possibly ask for."

He laughed. "Not even in England?"

"What about England?"

"Haven't you heard? The theater's in an uproar about it. The Comédie Française has been invited to play in London this summer *and* we're going," Mounet said.

{ 10 }

England! For months the *sociétaires* talked of nothing else. It was to happen in the summer because the theater had to close for repairs; only such a happy coincidence of events as repairs and an invitation had ever before taken the Comédie Française away from Paris.

Meantime life went on as usual.

"Have you seen the balloon in the gardens of the Tuileries?" Georges Clairin asked her. "No? People are thronging to it. You pay a price and then are allowed to sit in a little basket below the balloon and be hoisted up by ropes for a short flight. Of course the ropes are holding you fast to earth; you're perfectly safe."

Sarah was charmed at the idea. "Let's try it."

They went up several times for several days.

"But you still know you're tied to the ground by those ropes," Sarah objected after they had come down from one ride. "Wouldn't it be wonderful to really go sailing over Paris, with the balloon carrying us wherever the wind blew us?"

A man who was standing nearby, dressed in a uniform over-all, overheard her and turned to her. "Forgive my speaking to you, but aren't you Sarah Bernhardt? I am one of the pilots. I think I took you and your friend up yesterday. I just heard you say you would like to go up without the ropes. If you would, I could take you."

Sarah hesitated. "Would it be dangerous?"

Georges was sure it would be and said so. "There's no telling what might happen."

"It isn't as frightening as it seems," the pilot assured them. "I can always bring the balloon down when and where I wish by use of the valves."

Sarah was tempted. It was a brilliant spring day with just a slight breeze. The warmth of the sun was bringing out the first blossoms in the park, tulips were a brave show of red and yellow; overhead the sky was a clear, hard, bright blue. What a thrill it would be to rise high above the ground and be able to see all the familiar things in so unfamiliar a way. "Do let's go!" she begged Georges.

"All right." He was in love with her and could refuse her nothing. "But shouldn't you perhaps have on a warm coat?"

"On a day as mild as this?" She pulled the black twill jacket closer around her shoulders and flipped up the white starched collar so that it framed her face. With one hand she raised her skirts and with the other she took hold of the basket frame to help herself climb in. Georges settled himself on the little seat beside her. The pilot gave the last instructions to the ground crew, then the ropes were released and they rose swiftly, floating free and high.

The balloon, of course, had no motor power, no propeller, no steering wheel. The three in the basket were at the mercy of the winds except that by tugging on a rope from the basket to the balloon the pilot was able to adjust their flight a little.

It was a little scary at first. Sarah could look down on the startled faces upturned from the park and see their open mouths; she could see people pointing up with their fingers. Then she forgot the people and forgot to be scared; she gloried in all the beauty of Paris spread out below them. The balloon swung this way and that, lazily, in the breeze. She could see the river below and the boats on it, the spires of churches and the thick, pale green of the trees, the carriages like tiny toys on the streets that ran like spokes from the wheels of the Place Madeleine and the Place de l'Opéra.

"Look!" Georges pointed. "It's the Cathedral of Notre Dame."

For an hour the three of them pointed and exclaimed and called out to each other. Excited and happy, they sang songs and shared the biscuits and fruit the pilot had brought for his lunch.

Suddenly a strong gust of wind caught the balloon and sent it twisting up very high. The pilot did complicated things with the ropes, trying to bring them down, but the wind was rising swiftly, much too swiftly. A spring windstorm had hit Paris unexpectedly, in the matter of minutes.

The balloon was out of control. No one could blame the pilot. He could not have foreseen this treacherous change of weather on such a calm spring day. The wind swept them with terrific speed over the suburbs of Paris. It turned freezingly cold.

"I can't turn the valves too quickly or this wind will twist the balloon upside down," the pilot yelled to them over the rising crescendo of the storm. "I will have to turn them slowly and make allowances. I can bring it down all right, but it will take time."

Already numb and frozen, Sarah put her gloved hand up to her face to find that her nose was bleeding from the thin atmosphere and the altitude. There was nothing for them to do but huddle together and try to keep alive. It was bitter cold and both she and Georges found it necessary to keep their hands over their ears to try to stop them from aching.

It was midnight before the pilot finally managed to slowly lower the balloon to the ground. "But where are we?" They had climbed out and were stumbling around in the pitch blackness on half-frozen feet. Sarah was half laughing, half crying.

Dazed, they wandered around until they came to a railway station. It was a tiny one and the station master informed them that they were thirty miles from Paris and they would have to sit up all night in the station house because the next train wasn't due til morning. They had no food, and all had severe headaches from exposure. They could not sleep.

Yet they could laugh. The station master shook his head at the sight of those three sorry-looking strangers who seemed to find their predicament the subject for bursts of hilarious laughter that swept over them from time to time.

It was noon before Sarah reached home. Luckily she had had no performance the night before, but she did have a matinee that day. She just had time to change her clothes, eat, and run to the theater. Somehow she found the necessary strength to go on and the necessary fervor to play her part, but afterward she stumbled to her dressing room, sure that she would collapse and be ill.

Instead of being ill, she found she felt actually refreshed from

4/8/91

those two hours of acting. It was then that Sarah Bernhardt realized that, frail as her body looked, she was actually as strong as a horse and that work made her stronger instead of weakening her.

Her frailness had always been the subject of a lot of speculation and grave head-shaking and doubt that she would live very long. It even gave rise to jokes. One of the current jokes was that an empty carriage drew up to the door of the theater—and Sarah Bernhardt stepped out.

The balloon story caused a lot of talk backstage at the Comédie Française but it was soon forgotten in the approaching visit to London. Monsieur Perrin had much work to do, arranging a program for each performance, transporting costumes and scenery, and selecting the cast. This latter, of course was the job of the directors of each play and the Committee of Six.

Just when everything was going well, he thought, Perrin received a nasty jolt. The managers of the London theater had received his advance announcement of the first and opening night's program which did not contain in the cast the name of Sarah Bernhardt. Wires and cablegrams flooded the office of the Comédie Française: Sarah Bernhardt *must* play on opening night. The theater had been sold out on the strength of her name and reputation.

To Monsieur Perrin and the committee this was incredible. No one actress in the Comédie Française was that more important than the others. Back from London came more telegrams: we must have Mademoiselle Bernhardt for opening night.

There was no going against such a firm attitude. The cast for the two plays scheduled could not be changed but the committee compromised by inserting the second act of *Phèdre* between the two plays, just so that Sarah Bernhardt could be shown to the English public.

No one had realized that her fame had spread so far or that the London managers were counting so heavily on her name to bring people to the theater.

This was only the first shock. When they arrived in London it was Sarah Bernhardt the newspapermen wanted to interview; it was Sarah Bernhardt who was recognized and pointed out and cheered on the streets. The publicity about her in the papers threatened to eclipse the publicity about the rest of the Comédie Française until, as one *sociétaire* muttered, "We are just a background for her."

Opening night was one of those bad nights that an actress, no matter how talented, will have—even Sarah.

Everyone in the company was feeling strange and upset. Strange dressing rooms, strange surroundings, exits, and entrances in the wrong places, lights not fixed the way they usually were—all this made any normal nervousness more acute.

Sarah had the worst attack of stage fright she had ever known.

When her cue was given, she gathered up her long white robes and moved out from the wings into the full glare of the spotlights. Instantly the theater went into pandemonium. The audience clapped and yelled steadily for three minutes and the performance could not go on; the other actors stood around and waited while Sarah bowed and smiled, bowed and smiled.

And all the time the stage fright was growing worse. While she was bowing she was saying to herself, in a desperate vow to these wonderful people who were clapping, "Yes, yes, you will see—I will give you my very best . . ."

It was no use. As she took the first speech, she started off too high, her voice pitched too intensely. And once begun that way, it was impossible to stop. Every speech, every tone of her voice, every action was keyed too high, too loud, too strong. There were scenes when she wanted to speak almost in a murmur, plaintively; she wanted to vary the pitch and by so doing show more than one emotion. But she couldn't. She suffered, she wept, not only as Phédre was meant to suffer and cry but as Sarah Bernhardt conscious of giving a bad performance. When she begged Hippolyte for the love he denied her the words were torn out of her throat. When she said, "They love each other!" it was almost a shriek.

And the London audience loved it, went into raptures over it. They mistook her too-strained performance for a kind of acting that jolted them right out of their seats.

Even if all the theatergoers didn't understand French, though most did, they could follow the action of the plays. The Comédie

Française was a triumph on this tour. Londoners knew they were seeing great performers in great French plays, such as they seldom had a chance to witness.

As for Sarah Bernhardt, she became the rage of the city. Her clothes were copied; hats were named after her; her appearance in a carriage on a public street was the signal for stares—unusual in so reserved and polite a people as the English!—and for shouts of "That's Sarah! The Divine Sarah!" She was taken up by English intellectuals such as Oscar Wilde as well as by wealthy and important people who liked to be seen in her company.

All this was rather bewildering to her. She had been well known in Paris and her name was frequently in the newspapers, but she had never had such a fuss made over her before.

One night after a performance, while she was dressing to go out to a midnight supper, there was a knock on her dressing-room door. She picked up her crimson silk evening cape and flung it around her shoulders before she opened the door, expecting to see Mounet Sully, who was to take her to supper. Instead she saw two men who were complete strangers to her.

"Mademoiselle Bernhardt? This is an intrusion, I know, but would you be kind enough to give me a few minutes of your time? I am Edward Jarrett and this gentleman is Henry Abbey."

Though he spoke in French, his accent puzzled Sarah for a moment. Then she understood. "Oh, you are *Americans*? Your accent was not quite British, but I have met quite a few people from your country here, so I am beginning to notice the difference. Yes, please do come in."

She led them to two small, straight-backed chairs, removed her evening cape, and seated herself at her dressing table. "Now, what may I do for you?" She looked at each one carefully and was impressed by what she saw: Jarrett was tall, white-bearded, coolly, and most formally polite in manner; Abbey was magnetically handsome.

"Would you like to make a fortune, Mademoiselle Bernhardt?" Mr. Jarrett asked abruptly. His question would have seemed impertinent except that his manner of speaking was not.

She was taken aback. "Why, certainly." Of course she would

like to make a fortune. The house in Paris, all her extravagances, schooling for Maurice—these things cost a lot of money. No matter how good her salary was, she seemed to be constantly in debt. "But in what way, Monsieur?"

"By going to America." Seeing that she was about to protest, he put up a hand to stop her, and went on speaking. "I am a manager of *artistes*—actors and actresses. Mr. Abbey is the manager of some of the finest theaters in the United States. I asked him to come with me so that you would know our offer is a bona fide one. The offer is for you to make a grand tour of the United States and Canada. Mr. Abbey can guarantee you bookings in all of the larger cities of our country."

"But I do not speak a word of English. All my plays are in the French. Do American audiences understand French?"

"We have watched your performances here in London, Mademoiselle. It is not necessary to understand what you are saying to understand what you are doing, and why, and to feel the emotion you are portraying. The plot of the play can easily be printed in advance and will be a part of every program handed out to the audience," Mr. Jarrett said.

Something in his tone made Sarah realize that these two men were completely serious and that they had already argued and discussed every problem and question she would raise. But it was impossible!

"How would I talk to your newspapermen? Or to hotel clerks or anyone else?" she protested.

"Either myself or Mr. Abbey would be with you at all times to act as your interpreter."

There was a knock on the door and Mounet's voice calling to her.

"Please go ahead, Mounet," she raised her voice to say through the closed door, "and I will join you later. I am busy at the moment." Then she turned back to these two men who had brought such an exciting, if impossible, proposition. "But are you sure that the people in the United States want to see me? Would they come to see me act?"

Mr. Abbey, who had not spoken before, answered now. "They

will love you, Mademoiselle, even more than this London audience does. Our country is still new and young; many of the cities
have not had the opportunity of seeing really fine acting. Yet I
can assure you that nowhere in the world is the theater appreciated
and needed more. For that reason we can offer you more money for
this tour than you could possibly make in a year or more if you
stayed in France."

"There's no use even thinking about it," Sarah sadly replied.
"I am bound by contract to the Comédie Française. Of course, if
this were just a short trip perhaps I might ask for a vacation leave
from them. How long would this tour be?"

"Six months at least. You would need a month or two, I suppose, to select your own company and rehearse the plays you would
give; another month or more for traveling to America."

Her heart sank. "The Comédie Française will never grant me
the necessary leave."

Jarrett stood up, tall and distinguished and imperative. "Mademoiselle, in your position, one does not ask—one demands. Here
are my three addresses in New York, London, and Paris, where I
come from time to time. The day that you decide, càll me."

With courteous farewells they were gone.

Stunned, she listened to their departing footsteps. America! The
United States and Canada, those wonderful countries that everyone was talking about—bold countries, daring and young and already emerging as mighty forces in finance, invention, and science.
What would it be like to see them and act there? The French and
the English said there was no culture in the United States, yet
Mr. Jarrett and Mr. Abbey said there was.

Her heart was pounding. The money was a great temptation,
but that was the least of it. It seemed to her that it was a choice
between sitting like a caged sparrow in Paris or flying like an eagle
to America.

And what was it Mr. Jarrett had said of her—that one in her
position did not ask, but demand? Sarah was not vain but neither
was there any nonsense in her head about her own worth. She
knew he was right.

The offer was certainly something to think about, although the rest of her stay in England was such a whirlwind of events she hardly had time to think.

In order to raise money to cover some of her most pressing debts and bills, she had brought over with her some of her paintings and most of her finished sculpture. A small gallery was loaned to her for an exhibition and to her surprise the exhibition became one of the highlights of the London social season. The Prince of Wales came, the Prime Minister of England, crowds of English nobility and gentry in tall, pearl-gray top hats and canes and spats, the women in their finest afternoon costumes and jewels. When it was over, all of her works were sold and she was the talk of the artistic world.

Back home in Paris, Sarah said nothing of Jarrett and Abbey's visit to anyone except Madame Guerard. Her devoted companion did not try to advise her—she never advised—but she did say staunchly that if Sarah went then she was going too.

{ 11 }

The Comédie Française settled down to its usual routine. The theater reopened August 2, 1879. Sarah reopened in *Ruy Blas* and then in *Hernani*; both were solid successes again for her. But as the weeks and months went by she grew increasingly restless and moody. After the excitement of London she was having a hard time settling down. The Christmas season found her wishing desperately for something to happen.

"Mama, you're not listening to me." Fifteen-year-old Maurice, in his brand-new blue bathrobe, was trying to get her attention. He pushed her gently into a chair. "Look, I want to show you my Christmas present from Auntie Rosine."

While she exclaimed over the white silk scarf still in its bright Christmas wrappings, Sarah noticed with surprise how tall this son of hers was growing. Fifteen years old—it didn't seem possible. It meant that for fifteen years she had struggled upward on the long, hard road to success. Some might say she had reached the top in a very short time, but to her, remembering every heartache, every hour of disciplined study and work and deprivation, it was a long, long time.

She remembered the Christmas only a few days after he had been born. How terrible life had seemed to a young mother, penniless, alone, with a future possible to her only by her belief in her talent and her ability to work. Well, she had kept her vow to her son. He had not suffered from not having a father and now she was rich enough to see that he had good schools, good clothes, a horse of his own to ride.

All around her in the beautiful house so gaily decorated now for the holidays were evidences of the beauty and comfort she had created for him. They were in her lovely study. The day was drawing toward twilight; a white-aproned maid was pulling the heavy curtains over the windows. The butler brought in a heavy silver tray with tea cakes and sandwiches, the teapot for her and a mug of chocolate for Maurice.

The whole day had been wonderful, if exhausting, and she and Maurice were both glad now that all the guests were gone and they could have their supper together. Friends had come and gone since morning; there had been an informal party for six of her son's friends early in the afternoon.

It was pleasant, now, to sit and talk if they felt like it or be silent if they wished. Maurice had brought a book with him; she had a new play—*Froufrou*—to read for the first time. A fire crackled merrily in the great tiled fireplace. It was cozy and warm.

While Maurice drank chocolate with one hand and examined his new watch in the other, telling her in detail how much he liked it—"See? you wind it here and in the back I can open it and put a picture of you in it"—she looked at him and wondered, not for the first time, if it had been fair of her to have refused marriage with the Prince de Ligne.

Had Maurice suffered by that decision? Certainly she had given him love and tenderness and care. But perhaps the family would have relented and by now Maurice would have been the heir to the de Ligne name and fortune.

It was too late to worry about that. But was the temptation of America fair to him? It would be taking a terrific chance with their security. Here at the Comédie Française she was safe and so was he. Her contract was for twenty years and would undoubtedly be renewed after that.

If she could manage to curb her extravagances just a little, deny herself the new carriage, put off redecorating her studio, choose a less expensive school for Maurice's education, stop giving money to all her relatives—even the silk scarf from Aunt Rosine was paid for by her money, she was sure—if she could do all these things, then they could live within her income.

But if she did these things, she would not be Sarah Bernhardt. She had counted pennies once but it was not in her nature. She loved doing things in a big, lavish way; she was as reckless with money as she was with her life. She liked the feeling of being responsible for the happiness and comfort and welfare of so many people and knowing they all depended on her.

She thought, I wish I could confide in someone. If I could only discuss this with someone in the theater or someone with a sound business head. But of course I can't. If even a hint of it got out, I can imagine what an uproar it would cause in the office of the committee. She settled herself to the reading of *Froufrou*. Maurice settled down with a book.

They were interrupted by the butler. "There is a gentleman at the door who says it is most important that he see you, Madame. He said to give you this card."

She took the card, wondering what stranger could be calling at this hour on Christmas night. She glanced at the name on the card and her face turned white. "Will you ask the gentleman to wait for just one minute? Then bring him in here."

To the boy who was looking at her with wide-open eyes of surprise and dismay, troubled by something in her voice, she said, "Maurice, the man who has come to call on us tonight is your father." She handed him the card that bore the name PRINCE HENRI DE LIGNE on it. "You would not remember him nor will he remember you, though he saw you when you were a small baby. I must remind you, before you see him, in case you have resentments toward him, that he did want us to be a family. It was his father and his uncle who prevented our marriage——"

"And I only found out the truth a few years ago." The tall man who had spoken had entered the room before Sarah had realized he was there. "All these years I have been bitter toward you, Sarah, thinking it was the responsibilities of marriage you did not want. When I saw how famous you were becoming I was cynical. I thought it was flattery and admiration and applause that had prompted you to reject me. Now I know better." The handsome, distinguished gentleman turned to the fifteen-year-old boy. "And this is my son? Maurice?"

The two gravely shook hands. Maurice then moved a step backward so that he was standing close to Sarah.

Sarah and Henri looked at each other for a long time. The same thought was in both their minds: We are strangers to each other. Both had unconsciously carried around in their hearts a beloved memory of the other, a picture of each other as they had been fifteen years ago. Now they were changed. Now, though he was still a good-looking man, it was she who was the arresting and dominating figure in that room.

No longer was she the frightened girl he had comforted in the palace of Napoleon, nor the young girl so eagerly in love with him, no longer the brokenhearted young woman who had once sent him away from her shabby room. What she was now was the result of her own work, her own struggles, and it had made her into a personage while he had gone on just being what his life had meant him to be: a title, an aristocrat, a man who had done nothing of his own except manage his estates and live comfortably off his inherited money.

What they had done, what they were, was written in their faces.

She managed to smile. "Please sit down, Henri. I am sure you want to talk to Maurice and it will shortly be his bedtime."

While the father questioned his son about school, about his

playmates, about his life, she was questioning her heart. Was she still in love with this man? Even though she had cared briefly for others, she had never loved fully because the memory of Henri had been always with her and she had felt bound to him.

It was all over now, she knew. He was a stranger to her. The young man she had loved was gone.

When at last it was time for Maurice to go to bed, Prince Henri kissed him and held him tightly for a moment, to the boy's embarrassment. Then Henri turned to Sarah and said:

"You have done a good job with our son. He is a fine boy." He seated himself opposite her, propping his hands on the head of his walking-stick. "I had thought, Sarah, when I came here tonight, to ask you to marry me. I thought perhaps we could be a family. But now I see it would not be fair to you. You have given him everything that a father and a mother could give him. And what do I have to offer you?" He smiled. "Nothing. I am not really wealthy. My interests and my friends are dull compared to yours. I would be asking that you share with me our son, who is all yours now. And we are both proud people; I would insist on being the head of the family. For an ordinary woman that might be all right, but I cannot see Sarah Bernhardt meekly submitting to any husband's orders. No, I will not ask you to marry me—but we are friends, aren't we?"

Impulsively she reached from her chair to put her hand on top of his. "We are, Henri. For a while I was bitter at what your family had done to me, but now I think it was all for the best."

"Yes. To have become the actress you have, Sarah, there must have been a great talent in you always. It would have had to come out or else you would have been miserable."

Suddenly she felt comfortable and happy with him. Here was someone who might give her good advice, but who was not of the theater.

"May I confide in you a problem?" Then she told him of Jarrett's offer of the American trip and her confusions about it, the temptations and the doubts.

When she finished he was silent a moment. He looked at her with keen, thoughtful eyes, as if he were studying her closely. "My first answer would be: no. Don't go. You are with the finest acting company in the world—what else could you want? But you are an unusual actress. So many times in these years I have sat in a box and watched you and marveled at you. I think you have given these spectacular performances because you are self-willed and unafraid."

He tapped his shoe with his cane. "You have a fire, a drive, that others do not. If you were afraid to take chances with your life you'd be afraid to take chances with the way you act a scene. I don't think you can afford to trade that for security. Trust your own instincts in this matter, Sarah. This fire I speak of—it is as great a danger to let it smolder indefinitely and perhaps burn itself out by neglect than it would be to let it blaze too high. . . . But now it is getting late. I must go."

She walked with him into the hall and to the front door. A figure was sitting on a low bench in the dark hallway.

"Why, Maurice, I thought you were in bed? You haven't even finished undressing."

"I couldn't go to sleep."

The two older people exchanged glances. Naturally the boy was excited over his new-found father.

"Would you like to drive with me to the railroad station?" Prince Henri asked. "The driver will bring you back safely before he takes my carriage to my stables. I am leaving the city for my country estate tonight."

Sarah nodded and the boy hurried to put on his coat and hat. He went with his father, showing Sarah a face at the doorway in which there was a strange mixture of gladness, eagerness, and reluctance that she understood perfectly.

In the empty sitting room Sarah moved around slowly, picking up some of the Christmas presents still strewn around. She held the white silk scarf that Maurice had received from Aunt Rosine, smoothing it and folding it.

Henri had called her self-willed. She must have always been so, when it was something she wanted very badly. The memory of herself as a dirty little urchin seeing Aunt Rosine step out of that carriage, the glad recognition, following her aunt upstairs, seeing her give money to the nurse and then turn away and start to leave her—Sarah shuddered. Through her woman's body she could still feel the passion of wanting to go with Aunt Rosine, a passion that made terror and danger and falling out of a window nothing at all if it gained her what she wanted.

This trip to America was very much like jumping out a window. Just shut your eyes and jump? Risk everything—your reputation and all your future on such a reckless venture? But if the child Sarah hadn't jumped, Aunt Rosine would have gone off and left her. And if she didn't jump now, she would be imprisoned forever in the system and the rules and the routine of the Comédie Française.

In America she would be the star. It would be her company. She would choose all the plays, decide every move. In America there was adventure and novelty and—oh! what was the use of thinking about it?

But she had thought about it and though she didn't know it then, she had reached her decision. Somehow she was going to America.

The sound of a door banging and footsteps running toward her sitting room told her that Maurice had returned. He poked his head around the door. "May I come in for a moment?"

"Of course." She led him over to a sofa and they sat down together. "Now tell me, what did you think of your father."

He began to laugh. "Oh, I must tell you the whole story." The confusion was gone from his face. He turned toward her an open, smiling face and Sarah knew that everything was as it had always been between them. "On the way to the station, the Prince—my father"—he stumbled over the word—"began to tell me all about his estate in the country and all about his life. I think he must have liked me, because he was telling me over and over again what it would be like for me if I was his son and I would have his title and I would meet his friends . . ."

Sarah knew a quick and savage anger. How dared Henri do this behind her back, trying to win the boy away from her after telling her he was satisfied with her care of him?

". . . and that being a de Ligne would mean a lot to my future

111

career," Maurice went on, blithely, not seeing what was in his mother's eyes. "When we got to the station, it was terribly crowded with lots of people and we couldn't get a porter to carry his luggage. Then one of the porters looked at me and said, 'Aren't you Sarah Bernhardt's son?' He remembered us from the last time we went to the country. I said, 'Yes,' and he immediately took my father's luggage. So then the Prince looked at me and shook his head and said, 'You had better stay as you are. A prince can't get a porter, but Sarah Bernhardt's son can.'"

They both laughed and she hugged him. "And now Sarah Bernhardt's son had better go to bed," she told him.

That night marked an important new step in the relationship between mother and son. Maurice seemed to become all Bernhardt and, young as he was, began to take an interest in the theater.

The next afternoon he asked her about the play she was studying and begged her to read it to him.

"It's a little grown-up for you," she protested, "but if you want to hear it, very well. I'll tell you the story instead of reading it."

Maurice had just come in from school; now he put his schoolbooks down on a small table, drew up a chair so that he faced his mother, and folded his arms, looking at her intently.

As she began to speak, she was amused at his assuming so adult a manner, but she concealed her amusement. "*Froufrou* is very different—nothing like any play I've ever done before. It's about a pretty young girl, very sweet but foolish. Frivolous and gay, always wanting to have a party or a good time, to wear pretty clothes and be admired and petted and spoiled. She's always been treated as a child, so, even though she is grown up now, she still behaves as one. Little Froufrou knows that it makes people smile to see her bubblingly happy and it makes people feel good to treat her like a doll, so naturally she doesn't even try to be sensible."

"I thought you didn't like to play silly girls," Maurice objected. "They don't suit you."

Her amusement at her son vanished. He was being serious and what he said was sensible. "I don't as a rule. But let me tell you the rest. Little Froufrou gets married to a kindly, hard-working man who adores her and likes nothing better than to hear her laugh and watch her dance. He has enough money so that she can buy all the pretty clothes she wants and she can go to all the parties and balls and theaters. He spoils her more than her own family did. Even when their child is born, nothing is changed. Her older sister comes to live with them and this sister, Louise, takes on the running of the house and all the care of the baby. All Froufrou has to do is to amuse herself and be like a dancing ray of sunlight for the whole house. She is a happy child, a doll, not a woman."

"But it's not all her fault," Maurice interjected.

"Ah, that's just it. Gradually Froufrou begins to realize that she is not at all necessary in the house. Her sister Louise, who is secretly in love with the husband, is the real mistress of the house and is bringing up her sister's child. It is to Louise that the husband turns for companionship, not to Froufrou."

Sarah began to pace the floor, as she always did when she became excited. "Now comes the scene, a wonderful scene, and the only reason I want to do this play. Froufrou confronts her sister. She is jealous, though Louise has never been anything but good to her. Froufrou works herself up as she speaks, thinking out loud. It is a long, slow buildup of all the wrongs done to her; how she has always been treated as a child and never taught to be a woman. From mild reproaches Froufrou begins to think that Louise has actually betrayed her. And then, suddenly, Froufrou explodes into fury. She puts the whole blame on her sister. And what has been just a tiny quarrel becomes a tragic split between the two sisters and a tragic crisis for Froufrou. Now she cannot go back to what she was and there is no real place for her as a wife or mother."

Maurice was as excited as she was. "It's a wonderful part for you, Mother. I can just see you. That one scene would make all of Froufrou's world smash all around her!"

She laughed and came to stand beside him, stroking his hair. "Do you like the theater, Maurice? Do you think you would ever want to act?"

"No," he said thoughtfully, "not act. But I think I'd like to

113

choose plays for people and direct them when they act and maybe even write plays."

"Good. Maybe someday you'll write a play for me." And she kissed him.

Sarah was anxious to play *Froufrou,* but Monsieur Perrin did not care much for the play. Instead, he decided that after *Hernani,* sometime in March, she play Clorinda in *L'Aventurière* by Émile Augier.

The part of Clorinda was one Sarah hated. Also, in March, she had one of her very infrequent colds. She begged Perrin to drop the play or postpone it; she was feeling poorly and doing badly in rehearsals.

Perrin refused and the play went on. The next day the news-papers were ruthless in their criticism of Sarah—she could not remember when she had ever been treated with such scorn and ridicule. The critic of *Figaro* wrote: ". . . the new Clorinda, especially in the last two acts, moved her arms and body in a cheap, vulgar way which astounded us . . ."

This was too much. Sarah was in a fury such as she had not given way to for many years. She dashed off a note to Monsieur Perrin and sent copies of it to all the newspapers.

It read:

> You forced me to play when I was not ready. What I anticipated has happened. *L'Aventurière* is my first failure at the Comédie Française; it will be my last. By the time you receive this letter, I shall have left Paris. Kindly accept my resignation. Yours truly, Sarah Bernhardt.

{ 12 }

"But I don't understand it, Sarah." Mounet had caught her just as she was leaving the house. Her carriage was waiting. "You'd better come to your senses quickly, dear girl. To tear up your contract with the Comédie Française—why? Because one critic said you moved your arms and body in a cheap, vulgar way——"

"Never in my life," she flamed at him, "have I been cheap or vulgar!" She directed the butler as he carried out her luggage: "I'll keep my jewel case on my lap. You can stow the others away."

"But you did act badly. Why not face it? What actor does not have an off-night?"

Sarah had been waiting for Madame Guerard, now she moved down the steps. "I told you, Mounet, that I am going. I don't want to discuss it. Please forgive me, but I'm in a hurry." Then anger overcame her again and she stopped to face him. "It was all Perrin's fault. I wanted to play *Froufrou* and he wouldn't listen. He forced me to take the part of Clorinda and now I'm the subject of jokes and I'm called names."

Mounet walked behind them to the carriage. He felt the more disturbed because he was sure that Sarah was deliberately whipping up her anger rather than letting it cool off.

"Dear Mounet." She put her hand back to reach his. "Even if the others condemn me, you mustn't. If it hadn't been Clorinda, it would have been something else soon. Monsieur Perrin and I just do not see things in the same way. And I was getting sick of that treadmill."

She said a firm good-by so that he knew he must leave, though he was reluctant to do so. As he walked away, he thought, she gave herself away just then. It isn't just the anger over Clorinda. She is using it as an excuse.

The second he was gone Sarah turned to Madame Guerard. "I'm going into hiding, dear, and I'm leaving you the disagreeable job of handling all the messages that will be coming and all the people who will be clamoring to talk sense to me. You don't know where I've gone. That's all you can tell them." She looked with great affection at her old friend's quiet, placid face and at the hair that was beginning to turn gray.

Madame nodded. "I just hope Monsieur Perrin calls. I'll give him a piece of my mind."

Sarah laughed and picked up her jewel case. But as she was getting into the carriage she turned and said, "I almost forgot. If a tall, gray-haired man comes or sends a message; if his name is Monsieur Jarrett, then give him this." She handed her friend a sealed envelope. "It's my address."

Jarrett did come and he followed Sarah to her hideaway. She signed a contract with him for a four months' tour of the United States to begin that October of 1880.

When she returned to Paris a few days later the storm broke over her head.

Not until it was known that she had signed with Jarrett had anyone really taken her decision seriously. They all thought it had been a tantrum and that there would be a reconciliation between herself and Perrin and she would return to the fold of the Comédie Française.

The newspapers took sides: they called upon Perrin to apologize, they called on Sarah to apologize. They chided them both for behaving so foolishly.

Then came the terms of her American contract and the newspapers stopped treating the whole thing as a tempest in a teapot.

She was to have a salary of one thousand dollars a week; in addition, 50 per cent of all receipts at the box office above four thousand dollars. Two hundred dollars a week for hotel expenses. All the salaries of her company to be paid by Henry Abbey, who would be arranging her tour. While she was touring the American continent she was to have a private railroad car for traveling, which was to consist of a drawing room, a dining room, a room for herself, another for Madame Guerard, compartments with two beds each for her company, another for her staff, and a kitchen. The contract guaranteed a hundred performances in four months.

Since a thousand dollars, American money, was worth much more than a thousand francs, it was a contract to make all of Paris sit up and rub its eyes.

She was to select her own plays.

Now Perrin, realizing she was serious, came to see her and argue with her. She refused absolutely to change her mind, and his threat of a lawsuit over her breach of contract did not bother her in the least. A stream of people came at all hours of the day; some in outraged indignation at her, others pleading and begging, some sorrow-ing out of the fullness of their love for her.

For once in her life Sarah was not being truthful. She blamed Perrin. She would not admit, even to herself, that no one was to blame, that she herself wanted to leave.

She was thirty-six years old and she wanted to be her own master. She loved adventure for its own sake and new places ap-pealed to her restlessness. But it was more than that: if she was to try to reach new heights it could not be in the old way.

Threats, dangers, advice—she was turning a deaf ear to them. The newspapers warned, "Come back to the Comédie Française or you will lose the support of your French public"—"Come back or you will end up penniless and forgotten"—"Come back, Sarah, because we love you and you belong to us."

The theater did bring suit and the judgment was rendered against her. She must pay one hundred thousand francs. This was nothing. The American trip would pay for this easily, so easily she would never miss the money.

Luckily she was too busy to pay much attention to all the clamor. There was the company to gather together and rehearsals to hold. She had to choose her plays. There were all the details to be arranged by correspondence with Henry Abbey over scenery and stage props and lighting and costumes, many of which would have to be made in the United States.

There were personal matters to be settled. Maurice would stay with Aunt Rosine. The house would be closed for the four months; the horses must be stabled; furniture wrapped in dust sheets. Most of this Madame Guerard took care of but some of it fell on Sarah's shoulders.

The day of departure came. The company went to Le Havre to board ship and there Sarah found, to her joy and her tears, a great crowd of her friends. But it was not a happy farewell. Not one of these friends was but dubious and worried over what she was doing.

Just as she was boarding the ship she bought a newspaper from a boy who was selling them to the passengers. In her stateroom she read an article by Arsène Houssaye, who had once been general manager of the Comédie Française and was now a renowned journalist:

> Having spent five hundred thousand francs for her house in the Avénue de Villiers, Mademoiselle Sarah Bernhardt needs money; so she is leaving for America. Be careful, Mademoiselle: to great art these distant peregrinations are not congenial and it suffers from the deplorable habits which are derived from this traveling-circus existence, lived slapdash between the hotel which one has left and the new theater to which one is going. What sort of a haphazard public is this, which understands nothing of either your language or your genius? An elephant walking on bottles in a circus would be more to its taste. For a French actress, real wealth is the applause of French hands.

She looked out the porthole window and saw that the ship was under way. They were sailing. She went back to her chair and read on:

> Like the conquerers of old, this restless genius imagines that she has but to appear in order to conquer, to set up the flag of French Art at the other ends of the world. I greatly fear that she will soon have to give up her illusions. In vain she will cast the fire and flame of her talent before a public which, not being familiar with our masterpieces, will come to see her only in order to be able to say: "I was there."

This was a frightening warning. She could not help but take it seriously. She hadn't been frightened at the possible loss of her fame or the risk in security that she was taking, but she was suddenly oppressed with the thought that this venture might result in the loss of her skill as an actress. Would her art suffer from living in a slapdash manner? Would she stop trying hard to please when possibly her audience might be coming to see her, if Houssaye was right, out of curiosity only?

Fright was becoming real fear; fear was becoming panic. She felt as if she were choking, as if she were going to be ill, as if the earth were heaving beneath her feet.

Madame Guerard came in.

"Oh Madame, what have I done? I've ruined myself!" Sarah gasped, trying weakly to get to her feet and falling back into the chair. "I'm frightened, I'm scared——"

"Nonsense. You're seasick," said her practical friend and got Sarah onto the bed. She was seasick all the way across, miserably so. All she wanted was to be back in her own house in Paris where nothing rocked or swayed or lurched or dipped.

As the ship came within sight of the New York skyline, though, she recovered miraculously.

It was October 27, 1880, and it was eight o'clock in the morning. A great ship, *L'Amérique*, was coming into its dock and from the deck of the ship a group of excited men and women peered down on the city whose skyscrapers had already awed them.

"And so early in the morning to have such crowds about!" Madame Guerard pointed out to Sarah Bernhardt the masses of people on the docks and in the streets surrounding the dock. "I have heard that these Americans are busy people, but do you suppose New York is always this crowded and busy at such an hour?"

Sarah loosened the collar of her fur wrap. It had been cold coming in, but now the sun was shining, promising a brilliant day. She, too, studied the crowd with wondering eyes. Perhaps a few of these people down there might be coming someday to see her in a performance. What were they like, these Americans she had hear so much of?

Suddenly a band began to play.

"Sarah, it's the *'Marseillaise!'* Our French national anthem. And look—all those people are waving at us and trying to sing. Sarah, they are carrying banners!"

Now they could see the huge banners and read what they said: WELCOME, SARAH BERNHARDT and AMERICA WELCOMES SARAH.

Thunderstruck, Sarah and the rest of the company looked down on the tremendous crowds who had come here to greet her. Since the boat was late, they had been waiting patiently for a long time in the early-morning chill.

Tears came to her eyes. And when the band played "The Star-Spangled Banner" no one stood more proudly to attention than she did, with tears running down her cheeks and her voice husky as she tried to sing the unfamiliar words. With so much warmth and friendliness from these people, how could she be afraid?

The ship had anchored. She was close enough now to hear them

119

yelling her name and see that many of them were waving little flags—the tricolor of France and the Stars and Stripes of the United States.

The purser approached her. "Miss Bernhardt, there are a lot of gentlemen coming aboard to see you. We have reserved the big salon so that you may be welcomed by this delegation and interviewed by the newspapermen. And may I, as a Frenchman, also wish you very well on this tour?"

Smiling, crying, half beside herself with excitement and joy, Sarah received the delegation of over a hundred of New York's most important personages, city officials, theatrical people, and journalists. Speeches were made to her and she must reply to them; flowers filled the salon. All this took a lot of time, yet when she came down the gangplank the crowd was still waiting for her.

Just as she was leaving the ship, a little woman dressed in black, inconspicuous, unnoticed by the newspapermen, brushed by her.

"Who is that?" Sarah whispered to Madame Guerard.

"I met her on the journey coming over and at first, frankly, I thought this crowd and the ovation was for her, not for you. She is Madame Lincoln, the widow of the great American President."

Sarah's first thought was to call to the black-clad woman and to share the honors of this day with her, but Mrs. Lincoln was already gone, into obscurity.

There was nothing of obscurity about the journey from the ship to the hotel for Sarah Bernhardt. It seemed to her that all of New York had turned out to line the streets and watch her carriage pass. Flowers were tossed into her carriage; people stood on each other's shoulders to catch a glimpse of her.

Never would she forget these sight and sounds: the clipclop of the horses' hoofs on the pavement, the jingle of the harness, the shouts and cries of welcome in which her own name sounded so odd in this American accent, the shy delegations of little girls who stopped the carriage to present her with bouquets, huge pictures of her which she glimpsed in store windows, the informal, friendly way in which some of the people broke loose from the packed sidewalks to run alongside her carriage and shout greetings to her. She smiled until her face felt stiff; she waved until her arm ached.

At her hotel, her balcony window was so low that passers-by could, by standing on tiptoe, manage to peek in and see her and that's just what they did, by the hundreds.

"You must step out and speak to them from the balcony, Miss Bernhardt," Henry Abbey urged.

"Just once. Then I must take a nap."

"But you can't sleep with all that noise and racket outside."

"Can't I?" She stepped out onto the balcony, made a little speech which no one on the street understood but liked just the same, then came back and shooed everyone out of the room except Madame Guerard. In a few minutes Madame came out smiling, to where Henry Abbey was waiting in the sitting room.

"So you think she cannot sleep, Monsieur? Take a look in there."

He did so and was astounded. Sarah Bernhardt, with a crescendo of noise and shouting rising and falling outside her balcony, was sound asleep.

"How can she do it?" he asked.

"I have been with her a very long time." She led him back to a chair while she began to unpack luggage. "And I think it is the secret of her tremendous energy, this ability of hers to sleep anywhere, anytime, to take a little nap on a train or backstage, for ten or fifteen minutes and then wake up full of strength and refreshed again. You will see."

He did. An hour later Sarah was wide awake and ready to get down to business details with him. She found the business prospects to be very good.

"The Booth Theatre has been sold out here in New York ten days ago and seats sold for as high as forty dollars," he told her. "When we saw what a demand there would be, we simply put the price up every day and every day the box office was thronged."

Sarah smiled. "That's very flattering but I am puzzled. Do the Americans really care so much for the theater that they will spend so much money for it?"

"That remains to be seen. That depends on you. This initial sale has been due to publicity."

"Publicity?"

With a flourish he produced a thick, large press book in which were pasted column after column of newspaper stories and pictures —all about her. She took the book from him and looked it over, turning page after page. Her face was horrified.

"But it says here almost nothing about the plays we will be giving or the kind of theater art we are bringing to America. It's all about me and almost none of it is true! Mr. Abbey, I never horsewhipped another actress! I do not keep a menagerie of tigers and lions in my Paris home, as it says here. I do not sleep in a coffin every night. I do not bathe in perfume. No, Mr. Abbey, I cannot understand these stories and I do not like them."

A lesser man would have quailed before the fire in her eyes, but Henry Abbey only laughed. "Of course you haven't done all these things. Publicity is always an exaggeration, though you must admit there is some basis for these stories."

"How dare you?"

"You did," he went on, unperturbed, "once slap an actress at the Comédie Française? Well, the horsewhipping was just a news-paper editor's idea of making the story better. And a London man did once give you a leopard cub?"

"It was a little pet. I gave it away as soon as it grew up. And as for the coffin story—I never slept in one. At one time I was in a play that was famous for its death scene. I began to think a lot about death and at that time I still thought I was frail and not likely to live long. So in a morbid mood I ordered a coffin made. It was delivered by mistake to my house; there was no place to put it except in my bedroom for a while until I could have it stored. Someone saw it there."

"Nevertheless the story is that you sleep in your coffin. From my point of view it is a good story, good publicity." He rose and put his hands on the back of his chair so that he was looking down on her. "You must look at these things from a business point of view, Mademoiselle. You wear tight skirts because you like them, though every other woman is wearing great, wide hoops. You wear high collars when others are conforming to the fashion of low necks. All this makes Sarah Bernhardt vastly different from any other person in the world and it brings crowds out to see you and brings money into the box office."

"I am an actress, not a circus freak!"

He went on. "The people who have bought tickets to the Booth Theatre have come because of this publicity and because we have told them that you are a genius, the greatest actress of our times. But—and this is what is important—publicity will bring them into the theater; it won't keep them coming back. It won't ensure the success of your tour. In the end it will be your acting art and that alone, stripped of all the rest, which will decide whether America loves and respects Sarah Bernhardt or looks upon her as an outlandish novelty."

She sat silently thinking for a moment. There was much in what he had said that was distasteful to her. After having a dignified and revered position in Paris, here she was treated as a public spectacle. However, there was a shrewd and sensible side to her. These stories were awful; yet they had attracted that huge crowd at the boat and had sold all those tickets.

Henry Abbey pressed home his point. "This publicity is just the blaring of trumpets to attract attention to you. It will have nothing to do with your failure or success. Americans love a display and a big noise, but you can't fool them. They know the real thing when they see it too. Remember, you are here only for four months. You haven't time to build an audience—to play to a half-empty house one night and increase it to two-thirds the next and a full house the next. Publicity will bring them in; then it is up to you."

"Very well. I forgive you, but it must not happen again."

"Oh, but it must." There was something magnetic, something sweeping and open and direct about this man that left her breathless. Was this what it was like to be an American, she wondered?

"It must," he repeated. "I've planned a lot of stunts for you. For the next few weeks I am going to see to it that the name of Sarah Bernhardt is seen and heard and spoken by everyone in this city."

His enthusiasm was irresistible. She laughed and held out her hand. "Very well, Monsieur. I am ready for anything, just so long as you don't send me up in a balloon."

The publicity, once launched by Abbey and Jarrett, gathered momentum. Soap was sold with her name on it; there were Sarah Bernhardt gloves, Sarah Bernhardt stockings, Sarah Bernhardt

123

handkerchiefs—even Sarah Bernhardt cigars! She was photographed standing on top of a huge whale that had providentially washed ashore on a nearby beach just two days before. Cartoons appeared in the newspapers emphasizing her thinness, her flowing red-blonde hair, her French accent, her strange clothes.

In the name of publicity she had to conceal her outrage when impertinent reporters asked her when she took baths and how often, what she ate, what she drank, if she had really been a Catholic nun, what her jewelry was worth.

All this, of course, was just the prelude to her opening on November 8. She had to demand time from Abbey to be allowed to get on with her work of rehearsals and to get her company accustomed to a strange, new theater. She had to soothe the injured feelings of her actors and actresses when they found things to be so different here: no spacious dressing rooms, a different system of lighting, painted backdrops that looked like no Grecian palace or Spanish castle any of them had ever imagined.

She had decided to give *Adrienne Lecouvreur* for the first night and follow it with *Froufrou, Phèdre, Hernani, L'Étrangère*, and a new play called *La Dame aux Camélias*, written by Alexandre Dumas, fils. *La Princesse Georges* she would keep as a fresh play for the other cities.

The reaction to the opening night, from the standpoint of applause and demonstration and from the newspapers, was tremendous. Only Sarah knew that it was not. "They liked the play, yes, but they did not feel it," she told Henry Abbey. "When I am on the stage I always get a response from the audience. I can tell when they are simply enjoying a play as they were last night and when an audience enters into it with me emotionally."

She was more than disappointed. She was worried.

"We've failed," she confided to Madame Guerard. "Everything they told me in Paris is true. The Americans don't understand our language or our kind of acting. I should never have come. I have ruined my whole life and career because of my foolish recklessness. If an audience only 'likes' Sarah Bernhardt, then I am just another actress, that's all."

She might be in despair but that did not mean she would not

go on trying. *Froufrou,* the second offering, was received with a little more warmth, though only a little. The new play, *La Dame aux Camélias,* later known as *Camille,* was next. She had never given it before an audience and she was dubious about its reception.

That night Henry Abbey was standing at the back of the theater when the curtain went up. He was too restless, too worried, to sit calmly in the seat reserved for him. He preferred to stand back here, his elbows on the railing that separated the audience in their seats from the lobby passageway. Latecomers were going by, whispering to each other. An editor stopped to speak to him:

"Not quite the sensation you hoped she'd be, eh Henry? Oh, she's good, I grant you. That voice of hers can do things to your heart and nerves you wouldn't believe possible. But it's going to take more than a voice to make up for not understanding that French business she talks. I sure wouldn't call her any kind of a genius."

The knuckles of Henry Abbey's hands whitened as he grasped the rail. He had as much at stake—his own reputation—in this tour as Sarah did.

He glanced at the printed program in his hand as the lights began to dim all over the house. It carried a full résumé of the story. Helpless now to do anything about it, he suddenly wished very much that Sarah was not venturing out tonight in something new. Why hadn't she stuck to her old favorites? Who knew anything about *La Dame aux Camélias?*

The house was dark now. Gas flames flickered brightly in only one place: the footlights and around the sides of the stage, illuminating the curtain as it slowly rose.

Henry saw a Paris street scene—a café, a gay crowd with girls selling flowers, lovers walking arm and arm in the street, students laughing and talking at a table outside the café. The music of a hand organ was pertly, liltingly gay in the cool evening of a Parisian night.

In this scene Sarah appeared, as Marguerite, lovely in her frivolous, sophisticated gown decorated only with the camellias she loved. She was laughing, teasing lightly the man she was with,

125

hanging on his arm yet giving the impression that if another man appealed to her she might leave this one easily.

Even if Henry Abbey had not known the story, it was obvious that Marguerite was a flirt; charming, light-minded, will-of-the-wisp Marguerite whose friends were the pleasure-loving Bohemians of Paris and whose protectors were wealthy men lured by her beauty.

Then Abbey watched Marguerite meet Armand Duval, young, handsome, a student. There was a spark between these two, an electric something that made Abbey forget he was in a theater watching a play. For the first time a genuine emotion was on Marguerite's face.

A quickening ran through the whole audience. Sarah had triumphed over the language barrier—it needed no words to understand the little gesture she made of a hand touching Armand's sleeve, a look of wonder on her face, a new and different radiance in her eyes.

Armand, madly in love with her, begged her to leave this life in Paris and go to the country with him. Let the two of them be alone where what they felt for each other might have a chance to become real love. Here in Paris love was a mockery.

Watching the play of emotions on Marguerite's face—the wistful yearning, the unsureness, the temptations of money and jewels and parties in Paris compared to the simple life Armand was offering her—Abbey found himself pleading with her silently. Go with him, Marguerite!

Abbey, shrewd businessman, hardened theatergoer, had completely forgotten that he was watching a play.

He saw the two lovers in the country now, where Marguerite and Armand were happy in the splendor of their love. How beautiful she was, her frail pallor gone in the health of this life!

Then, one day, while Armand was absent from the cottage, his father appeared. Stern and hard, the old man reproached Marguerite. She was ruining his son. Because of her, Armand would have no career, his fine name was being dishonored. Disappear from his life, the father commanded her.

As Marguerite wept, Henry Abbey found his eyes filling with tears and he wanted to protect and shelter her.

She returned to Paris to a former admirer and here at a gay party, Armand found her—to all appearances once again caught up in her wasteful, useless life, with no thought of anything but pleasure and money. She was frail and pale again, her skin as waxen as the camellias she still wore.

Her first look at Armand was one of unutterable love—then she remembered. She must play her part. She must not let him know that she had sacrificed their love for his sake. Her face changed; she became the taunting flirt.

Enraged, Armand flung her to the floor. He threw money at her and called on all the guests to come and gaze upon the woman who had no heart and no soul.

The insult was too much for Marguerite's frail spirit and body.

When the curtain rose again, she was in bed, dying. A letter from Armand's father arrived telling her how much he has regretted what he has done and acknowledging the nobility of her sacrifice. The letter was followed by Armand himself. He threw himself on his knees by her bed. Forgive me for my lack of faith in you, he begged. Now our lives will be happy once more, now that we are together again.

It was too late. Marguerite knew it was too late.

The words echoed in Abbey's heart. Tears ran down his cheeks and he did not even bother to brush them off. All through the audience both men and women were sobbing.

But if too late for life, Marguerite told Armand, it was not too late for happiness. And Henry Abbey himself felt suddenly exalted by the great, sad joy in Marguerite's face as she knew that she was truly loved at last, was worthy of that love, was free of her frivolous shallow self and experiencing an emotion she had never known before.

She died—with a smile on her face and camellias in her hands, with Armand's kiss still warm on her cheek.

For a long time the audience sat, just as Henry Abbey stood motionless, unable to move, unable to bring themselves out of that Paris attic room into the present world of New York City and the

Booth Theatre. They had forgotten where they were, that it was a play they had seen.

Then they awoke slowly to the realization of the miraculous thing that had happened to them. First came a faint splatter of handclaps here and there; a cry of excitement rose from the balcony; then the noise spread into a wild, shouting, stamping pandemonium of applause.

The curtains parted and Sarah stepped forward, still in her costume. She led the whole company out into a line in front of the footlights. The house was in an uproar. For so long she had wrought such havoc with their emotions that they must have an outlet for them. They had watched genius and they knew it. Over and over again, until she was dropping with fatigue, she came back to receive the ovation they were giving her.

Several over-enthusiastic people leaped up onto the stage to embrace her. The theater rang with cries of "Sarah! Hurray for Sarah! Sarah Bernhardt! Marguerite!"

Henry Abbey made his way backstage, the businessman in him rejoicing. His gamble on her had proved itself to be a success. If she could act again as she had tonight, she would have all of America in the palm of her hand.

When at last she came back to her dressing room, white and tired but recuperating swiftly, he told her what he had been thinking.

"If you can do again what you did tonight, Miss Bernhardt, your triumph in America is assured." he said, helping himself at her invitation to the supper her maid had brought in.

"I can only try," she said. "What you are asking is more than has ever been asked of any actress. I realized that last night when I was reviewing the other two performances and wondering what was at fault. You see, in Paris I am accustomed to sharing the success of a play with the author. A spoken line—the words themselves—can be powerful enough to create emotion in the audience. Here I must do it all myself. Myself and the rest of the company, that is."

She was eating with an enormous appetite and once again he

realized how great a physical strain such an evening's performance must be on her.

"It must almost be pantomime, except that the voice will be just as important in carrying a tone, a subtle or a loud appeal to the heart. The acting will be in the tone of voice and in the gesture and in the face and body. It is a great challenge to an actress, Mr. Abbey. I can tell you one thing: if I succeed I will be ten times the actress after America that I was when I came here."

She continued: "It will be much more work and many more rehearsals for my company to learn to act in this new way. But you will see. Now I am confident."

Her confidence proved itself. The New Yorkers not only wanted to see *La Dame aux Camélias* over and over again, they also appreciated and were thrilled by the much more involved plots of *Hernani* and *Phèdre*.

Altogether, her company gave twenty-seven performances in New York and when she left for Boston, the newspapers were unanimous in appraising the performances as incredibly beautiful, tremendously popular. They next went to Boston where their ten-day run was equally a triumph. Next came Hartford, Connecticut, then Montreal, Canada. From there they went to Baltimore, St. Louis and Cincinnati.

Everywhere they found the same huge crowds waiting to welcome them, the same packed houses, the same ovations, applause, and admiration.

But it was an exhausting, grueling trip. No sooner were their engagements finished in one city than they must pile into the train and be off to another. Every week, or sometimes every day or two, the company had to get used to a strange theater; sometimes the stage was too small for the scenery, or else the actors found themselves straining to be heard in a barnlike theater so vast they could hardly see the balcony seats. Exits and entrances were all different and action had to be improvised according to the problems encountered in each theater.

They had to snatch moments to rehearse, moments to rest and relax. Each city tried to outdo the other in banquets and public affairs for them. Sarah loved them for their kindness but sometimes it was overwhelming. A gentleman in Boston brought famous masterpieces of painting and sculpture from his private gallery to hang all over the walls of her hotel suite—which was something like living in a museum, Sarah thought.

Edward Jarrett caught up with the traveling company in Cincinnati.

"I don't like to disturb Mademoiselle Bernhardt," he said to Madame Guerard in the hotel lobby, "because I know she needs her rest before leaving for New Orleans tomorrow. But I do need to discuss some small business matters with her. Would it be possible for you to awaken her?"

"She is not asleep. She is working."

"But she just finished a matinee performance!"

"Nevertheless. Come with me. We will go to my room, which is next to hers. We will watch from there and I will know the moment when I can interrupt her," Sarah's faithful friend and watchdog told him.

"When you say she is working, what do you mean?" Jarett asked, following her up the stairs.

"She works all the time. Frequently she reads new plays: playwrights are constantly sending her their work hoping she will like them. Every morning she writes to her son; then there are business and personal letters to Paris. Everyone in the cast brings her his problems and she must take time to discuss them. Someone's luggage has been lost, someone is homesick . . . I try to take much of this kind of burden off her shoulders, but it is always to Sarah they turn."

"But can't she rest now, after a performance?"

"Sometimes, yes. But what she is doing right now is the most important work of all. Last night she told me she was worrying about her portrayal of Phèdre. Something was lacking in it. She was not being the same Phèdre as she was that winter of eighteen seventy-four when she played it so well." Madame Guerard smiled as she halted outside her door. "So she is now trying to find out what is wrong."

She put her finger to her lips, opened her door quietly. They tiptoed in and she motioned him to a seat where, through a half-opened door, he could see into Sarah's sitting room.

Sarah was standing before a tall, pier-glass mirror, a book in her hand. The table beside her was piled high with books.

She turned, unaware of them, walked a few steps away from the mirror. She put down her book. Then, from her usual straight-backed posture she seemed to shrink a little, to become that soul-sick, tortured, worn figure of Phèdre. She moved toward the mirror, looking to one side as if she were speaking to someone:

> "O malice of great Venus! Into what madness,
> What wild distractions, did she cast my mother!"

Sarah shook her head and repeated the lines again, this time with strong emphasis on the words "great Venus."

She appeared to be half listening to someone's reply, half absorbed in her own thoughts.

"It is her will" Sarah's figure straightened. In the mirror Jarrett could see her face and the expression of fatalistic doom, of a woman not responsible for her own actions. Caught up in the excitement of her interpretation, Jarrett unconsciously made a sound of approval in his throat. Sarah heard it, stopped, and turned around. For a second there was flashing anger in her eyes, which vanished when Madame Guerard bustled quickly through the door, apologizing and explaining.

"It's quite all right," Sarah assured her. "I've found out what the trouble was."

Jarrett glanced down at the books on the table. Greek history, books on Greek myth . . . his eyes widened.

"Must you do this kind of research?" he asked.

"Did you think acting was a gift? That one reads a part and by some inspiration the imagination tells me how to become a Phèdre? If I only used my imagination then Queen Phèdre would probably behave on the stage like Queen Victoria. No, she belongs to a certain period, a certain country. Love and hate, duty and religion—all were looked upon in a very different way at that time."

131

Jarrett looked down at the floor. "I am ashamed," he said. "I am ashamed of the cheap publicity that Abbey and I have subjected you to. I hadn't thought of what a real artist you are, what a hardworking, dedicated woman you are."

She laughed at him. "Don't be ashamed. Once over the shock, I find I enjoy it. There's something in me that likes what you Americans call the 'razzle-dazzle.' In fact, I like Americans. I am so much like you. Americans never say anything is impossible."

❈{ 13 }❈

The next morning their train pulled out of Cincinnati for New Orleans. It had been raining steadily for days. Streets were a sea of mud. In the fields nothing could be seen of the earth, and the trees seemed to be standing in dirty lakes of water. Water splashed up over the railroad ties; the rain had swollen every creek, every river, until they were rushing torrents.

Sarah glanched out of the train window indifferently. Her mind was far ahead of the train, thinking about this new city of New Orleans and wondering what it would be like. What new complications would be waiting for her there? Would the lighting be adequate. How many dinners would she be expected to attend? She had heard that there were excellent restaurants in New Orleans where the company could get some real French cooking. She hoped so; it might help to smooth away some of the homesickness people in her cast were feeling.

They were approaching a bridge, she saw. At that same moment she also noticed that the train was slowing down and finally grinding to a halt. They were miles from nowhere, with no town in sight. Before she could understand what was happening, Jarrett and the engineer came into her car.

"Madame," the engineer began, too upset to care about polite courtesies, "we must turn back. That bridge is going to collapse any minute; it's dangerous to try to cross it. I'm not going to take the responsibility—not unless the lady insists upon it."

"But we must be in New Orleans tonight. Besides, I thought Americans didn't consider anything impossible."

Jarrett translated for both of them. The engineer shrugged his shoulders. "If you insist . . ."

"How great is the risk?" she demanded.

"I don't know. I can't tell a thing about it, for sure. I just know it looks bad. Those bridge supports never were very strong and I can see them shake now every time the water slaps against them. If we must go on, all right, but I have a wife to think about. We just got married and I'm not going to leave her a widow without a cent. If you'll wire her twenty-five hundred dollars right now—I'll take a chance."

Impetuously Sarah agreed. The engineer backed the train until it reached a small station; Jarrett got out to wire the twenty-five hundred dollars, in Sarah's name, to the engineer's wife. Then the train started forward again.

She was amazed at the speed they were traveling at; the train rushed forward and it seemed to her to be going so fast that surely the cars would leap off their rails. She could hear the excited clatter of tongues from the next compartment. Madame Guerard came running in to find out what was happening.

At that moment, too late, Sarah realized what she had done. In her own love of excitement, at taking a chance, she had not thought to consult with the others. She was deliberately endangering not only her own life, which she had a right to do, but also the lives of thirty-two people who had nothing to say about it.

She remembered, with a sickening sense of guilt, Mother Sainte-Sophie saying to her, "Sarah, dear child, will you never learn the difference between courage and sheer senseless recklessness?"

The train almost flew over that bridge. Above the sound of the clicking wheels and the churning water below, Sarah could hear something even more ominous: the creaking and the breaking, the *actual* breaking, of wood! The splintering, groaning, crack of timbers collapsing.

The train made it across. But only in split seconds before the bridge completely collapsed with a tremendous roar. Great billows of water gushed up as from a fountain. Huge jagged fragments of wood shot up into the air and then crashed back into the boiling stream.

The engineer was wise enough not to stop and let any of the passengers see what had happened. He just kept going ahead and soon the excited questions and the horrified speculations among the people on the train ceased.

Only Sarah still sat, trembling, her hands covering her face. She might have caused all of these people to die. Would she never learn that there were some challenges best left alone?

It was New Orleans for a whole week, then Mobile, Alabama, the next day and on through the South and the Middle West, playing in small town halls and big city theaters. Everywhere the audiences genuinely loved the plays and were moved and excited by the acting. Sarah saw that what she had predicted was true: she and the whole company were being forced to raise their acting to a newer and higher standard to cope with the problems of language. They were developing the power to tell a story in a single gesture, an action, the inflections of their voices.

When the tour was finally over—six months was too short a time to cover the far West—their thoughts turned now to Paris. Henry Abbey was reluctant to see them go. The tour had been financially more successful than anything he had dreamed of. He would have liked to keep them longer, but Sarah was as anxious for Paris as was her company.

They were accompanied to the boat by a bigger crowd than had greeted them. Once again the band played the *"Marseillaise"* and "The Star-Spangled Banner." Thousands of people shouted, "Come back, Sarah!"

She reached Le Havre on May 17, 1881, and was met by Maurice. He had grown taller and more dignified, no longer quite the young boy she had left. All the way on the train to Paris she told him excitedly about America, about the tour, about her plans for her next appearance on the stage of Paris. Never had the countryside of France been more beautiful to her eyes than at this moment. Fresh from her American triumphs, she was returning confident and happy about the future.

She hardly noticed how silent Maurice was, or the way he held her hand tenderly, almost protectively.

When she arrived at the Paris station she looked about her, surprised. True, she hadn't expected the kind of crowds that had thronged every railway station in America, but she had expected some kind of a reception. There was no one here.

Still wondering, she thanked the rest of the company and dismissed them, knowing how eager they were to see their families. Then she and Madame Guerard and Maurice took their carriage, which was waiting for them, and drove to their home in the rue de Villiers.

It was a welcome sight, this house of hers, but again she was struck by the absence of little things she had always seen when she returned: flowers sent by admirers, notes of congratulations, invitations piled high on the hall table, the doorbell ringing with friends coming to see her. She examined the very few letters, looking particularly for one from a Victorien Sardou, a playwright. She had agreed before she left America to act in his new play.

There was nothing from Sardou. Now she was forced to admit that something was strange, that there was something most unhappy about Maurice's attitude.

"What is it, my dear? What is wrong?" She led the way into her drawing room and went first to the windows, flinging them wide open to admit the lovely spring air.

When Maurice remained silent, she grew impatient. "Come, tell me. Something is wrong and I must know."

"It's just that—you say that America was a success for you—but the newspapers are saying that it isn't so," he blurted out. "They have been saying awful things about you and printing terrible pictures."

"What kind of pictures?"

"There's one of you on a whale and the story says this is what the once-great Sarah Bernhardt is good for now—to stand on the back of whales. And there was another one of you with a shower of gold coins coming out of your mouth. Underneath, it said that instead of having a golden voice now, it's just the tinkle of gold coins that the audience hears. They say you have become so mad about money that you aren't an actress any more. There have been stories that the audiences in America cried in the wrong places and laughed in the wrong places because they didn't know any better and you didn't care, as long as they paid to see you."

"So that is what they are saying." Sarah stormed up and down the large room. "That I am money-mad. Do they say anything else?"

"Yes. That you are finished. You couldn't get an audience in Paris because Paris wants to see acting, not freaks." He gulped. "I don't care what they say. I know it isn't true. The other fellows in school bring those pictures and laugh at them . . ."

Now she was really angry. That her son should have been exposed to this humiliation! "Let me see some of these newspapers."

Maurice went to fetch them. While he was gone her anger grew but at the core of it was bewilderment. Jarrett, acting as her personal manager, had sent long stories back to Paris telling the newspapers how triumphant her tour had been. How could things have become so distorted?

When she read the clippings she was even more puzzled. The tone of them was not critical, as it had been when she left the Comédie Française. They *pitied* her now.

Poor Sarah Bernhardt [one article read]. Poor passionate lover of fame! If she sinned by loving uproar too much, she has been well punished over there. Mademoiselle Sarah Bernhardt went to the United States to capture everything—hearts, applause, bouquets and, especially, plenty of money. Mademoiselle Sarah Bernhardt, humiliated and angry, has had to renounce her success in the drawing rooms as well as in the theater, where her noisily announced performances take place in half-filled auditoriums of people who do not understand them. It was for this pitiable result that she threw her contract as a *sociétaire* of the Comédie Française in M. Perrin's face! Poor Sarah Bernhardt!

"I cannot understand this." Sarah crumpled the newspapers into her hands. "Such lies! By why——?"

"I think I understand," said Madame Guerard in her usual common-sense way. "You hurt people here when you left as you did, Sarah. They did not want you to succeed in America and now they believe what they want to believe."

"Well, we'll soon tell them the truth."

"How—if they wouldn't believe the reports of Monsieur Jarrett? No, we French are obstinate. Once we get an idea firmly fixed in our minds we don't change easily. If you were to send a letter to the newspapers now they would just shake their heads and say, 'Poor Sarah, she has crept back to Paris to lick her wounds and now she wants to pretend that everything is all right.'" Madame Guerard was blunt.

More than anything else that convinced Sarah was the fact that Victorien Sardou was obviously shunning her. The playwright had been so anxious for her to act in his new play, *Fédora*; he had written and cabled. But he had stopped writing and cabling more than two weeks ago and now there was this absolute silence from him.

She waited for a few days. Not a word came from either Sardou or from the manager of the theater, Monsieur Deslandes. They were avoiding her. They no longer could trust *Fédora* to Sarah Bernhardt, who had been branded a failure.

It would not do for her to lower her dignity by going to see them. She could have rented a theater and put one one of her old favorites, but with Paris in this strange mood, would anyone come? And if they did come, might it still not be disastrous? She knew enough of audiences to know that if an entire theater was filled with hostility, this transmitted itself to the actors on the stage. And sometimes a hostile audience would see in the finest performance only its small flaws and little mistakes.

That which had damaged her most, in Parisian eyes, was her new style of acting. She had learned in America how best to use gestures and tones. But the Paris newspapers now said she had lost all subtlety, that she could not speak quietly or softly, that she now used tricks of gestures instead. They claimed she had become an acrobat, not an actress.

"Something bold, something spectacular, that is what I need; something to shock them out of this attitude," Sarah said to Madame.

When the idea came to her it was not only bold—it was reckless, ever unscrupulous.

{ 14 }

On July 14, the great national holiday of France, there was to be a grand performance at the Opéra. The president of the Republic of France would be there, along with every other notable in the country. This was the tenth anniversary celebration of the liberation of French territory from the Germans. It had significance in every patriotic French heart.

The Opéra celebration was to consist of three acts of a favorite opera by Meyerbeer, interlude performances by members of the Comédie Française, and many other special appearances. Sarah, with her true sense of what was most melodramatic in this celebration, had her eye on the one event of the evening: the recitation of the "Marseillaise."

It was to be given by Madame Agar—the same Madame Agar who had played Sylvia to Sarah's Zanetto in Le Passant. Madame Agar was now fifty years old, an established actress with a comfortable, secure position in the Paris theatrical world.

Sarah argued with her conscience. To miss this performance would mean little to Madame Agar, while to have this chance was a matter of life and death for her own career. Her conscience needed little persuasion.

138

And Sarah knew Agar's weakness. The aging actress was always, forever, impetuously, in love. At this moment it was a captain in the Army.

Early on the evening of the fourteenth a message came to Madame Agar. Her captain was in Tours and he had just been hurt in a fall from his horse. Could Madame Agar come? Forgetting her duty to the theater, her patriotism—everything— Madame Agar forthwith bundled herself into a carriage and was off for Tours.

Outside the opera house, a carriage waited beside the stage door. A figure sat in the carriage and bided the right time, hooded and cloaked so that no one could recognize her. A copy of the program was in Sarah's hands. Every now and then she glanced at it: now they were performing the opera by Meyerbeer. It was still too early. Wait for the right moment, just after the special performance by Mounet Sully.

Timing was all-important. If Agar's absence was discovered or her own identity uncovered too soon, it might still be possible for the producers to push in another substitute. The *"Marseillaise"* was the last event of the evening.

Slipping out of the carriage, she wrapped herself tightly from head to foot in her long cloak, pulled the black velvet hood over her hair and forehead so that her whole face was shadowed. She walked through the backstage door, past the doorman who might have stopped anyone else but who was impressed by the imperial gesture she made to him and her confident manner in brushing right past. He opened the inner door for her.

She breathed fast but a little easier now. The first hurdle was over. She was at last in the backstage of the Opéra.

Here it was dark—dim, rather. Only a few tiny lights flickered; people moved past each other without recognition. She had counted on the excitement of the occasion. People were too busy to be curious about one another.

Mounet Sully and another member of the Comédie Française were on stage now, giving the last scene of their play. Slowly she moved closer, closer, closer to the wings immediately adjacent to the stage. Nothing was going to stop her now!

There was a great roar of applause from the audience. The act was finished; the two members of the Comédie Française were coming offstage. The first one brushed by her. But the second was Mounet Sully and no disguise of a cloak or hood could hide from him the figure and face of Sarah Bernhardt.

"Sarah! What are you doing here?"

At his cry, others stopped and stared. One of the producers of the show was standing nearby and came rushing up.

"What are you doing here? Are you watching the show from here rather than from out front? It's perfectly all right, Mademoiselle Bernhardt—honored to have you . . ." he stammered, perplexed.

But Sarah was speaking to Mounet. "Good evening, Jean," she said. "Would you mind holding my cloak?"

She whipped off cloak and hood with a regal gesture. A gasp went up from everyone around. Sarah stood revealed in the classical costume that all actresses in France wear as a symbol of the Revolution and the *"Marseillaise"*—the long, white gown girdled with the sash of three colors, and the black hat on her head with its wide, wide wings.

"But I don't understand!" the producer sputtered. "What are you doing—where is Madame Agar? Someone go to Agar's dressing room and tell her she is late; it is time for her to go on."

Sarah smiled at him. "Oh, I'm sorry, I was forgetting. Poor Madame Agar. She had to leave Paris an hour ago, having been called urgently to the bedside of a sick friend. She sends her apologies and I am to take her place."

Then seeing that the news had left the producer dumbfounded and wanting to take advantage of this before he recovered his senses, Sarah moved quickly. She picked up the folds of her gown and walked quickly toward the stage, saying over her shoulder, "I need hardly say that I am very glad to oblige you."

The producer reached out a hand to stop her but it was too late.

The musicians had caught sight of her just inside the wings, and as she moved onto the stage they struck up the first bars of the *"Marseillaise."* Sarah's audacity had caught everyone by surprise; there was nothing anyone could do now to stop her.

140

She moved with her incomparable grace to the center of the stage. She took the flag from its standard and raised it high in both of her hands, then stood silent for a moment before the audience.

Everyone rose, following the lead of the president of the Republic. The house was still silent except for the music playing softly. Then slowly people again took their seats.

Sarah began to speak. Quietly, with a deep and glorious intensity, she uttered the words:

> *"Allons, enfants de la Patrie,*
> *Le jour de gloire est arrivé. . . ."*

"The day of glory has arrived!" Her magnificent voice filled every corner of the huge opera house even though she was still speaking in that low tone, letting each word come out with a slow, measured passion that sent shivers down the backs of her audience.

She was using her voice as she had never used it before, as she had learned to use it in America, so that, standing perfectly motionless, she was creating a havoc of emotion in every heart.

> *"Aux arms, citoyens! . . ."*

The whole audience was spellbound, caught up in a thrilling embrace of patriotism. No one moved. No one coughed or even sighed. Everyone held his breath, fearing to miss one syllable of that voice reaching out to them with its golden cry for victory. Hard lumps formed in every throat, a choking sensation in every breast, as her voice changed from that low tone to a ringing cry. That white-clad figure on the stage was the symbol, the embodiment of France. Gladly would they have followed her anywhere, into battle or to the ends of the earth.

Once again she raised the flag on high in both her hands and as she sang out the last lines of the *"Marseillaise"* it was as if a great bell were ringing, tolling its pure music over their heads and into their hearts.

It was over.

She had brought them to such a pitch of ecstasy that when the reaction came it was not applause—it was tumult. Men shouted

141

and women cried out; the president stood up and bowed to her, too overcome to hide his own tears. "Bravo! Bravo! Bravo!" "Encore, Sarah Bernhardt! Encore!"

Even the producer waved to her to recite it again.

She was forced to repeat it, not once more, but twice, from beginning to end before the audience was satisfied and would let her go. She had furnished one of those exceptional, exquisite moments when the best in the theater had united with the best emotions of France.

And as for Sarah, this time her recklessness had won the day. In that one stroke she had recaptured her popularity and her reputation in Paris; she had confounded every falsehood said against her. Once more she was recognized as Sarah Bernhardt, an actress of genius.

Even good-natured Madame Agar, who had always been fond of her, forgave her for the trick. She had found her captain well and sound and that was sufficient to soothe her feelings.

Now Sardou and the manager Deslandes brought her their new play *Fédora*. Riding high after her triumph and inclined to punish them a little, Sarah was not quick to sign with them. To their astonishment she announced that she was going on tour of the French provincial cities first, then perhaps a tour to Russia, where she had just been invited to appear in Moscow.

Sarah Bernhardt was on top of the world. She was the Divine Sarah. France, England, the United States, Canada—all recognized her genius and called her the greatest of actresses. She could have any play she wanted, any theater (with the exception of the Comédie Française, which she did not want). Life had never seemed so wonderful to her. There were no new worlds she could not conquer—and being Sarah, she could not help looking for new challenges.

In this mood and at this time Jacques Damala came into her life.

No sooner had she returned from her very successful tour of the French cities and towns than she felt she must give a party, a lavish affair to which she would invite all her friends. She did not hold it against any of them, not even Mounet Sully, that they had not rallied around her when she first returned from America. She knew they had been embarrassed; they had believed the stories and had not wanted to come to see her out of pity.

The night of her party her house was perfumed with flowers, splendid in its beautiful decorations. It seemed that every minute another carriage or hansom cab drew up at the door and the butler opened the door to another of her friends: actors, actresses, political figures, artists, writers, journalists. Francisque Sarcey was there—Monsieur Duquesnal—Georges Clairin, still in love with her—Edmond Rostand, François Coppée, Sophie Croizette. Even the great Victor Hugo made a quick appearance, leaving early because he was not well.

Sarah, seated in her drawing room, looked across its loveliness, over the heads of this gay crowd chattering and laughing and talking, and saw a man who was a stranger to her.

She caught her breath at the sight of him. Jacques Damala was so handsome that he made even the good-looking Mounet Sully look ordinary by comparison.

"Who is he?" she whispered to a friend.

"The man who looks like a dark Greek god? That's Jacques Damala. Stay away from him, Sarah. He has a bad reputation. I believe he's Greek by birth; at least I know he is a member of the Greek diplomatic service here in Paris. He has many friends among actors because it is said the only thing he wants in life is to be an actor himself. But I've heard many unpleasant stories about him. They say he is hard and cruel and breaks the heart of every woman he knows."

Sarah's interest was caught, but she had her duties as hostess. For a while she was busy greeting people, embracing with pleasure the lovely Marie Lloyd, chatting with Georges Clairin who looked distinguished in his evening clothes, curtsying with profound, genuine affection before Victor Hugo. Then, for a few minutes, as the little groups reformed themselves around the room, she was standing alone.

It was then that Jacques Damala came up to pay his respects to his hostess and be introduced to her. To her amazement, she saw that that was all it was to him—a duty. He bowed in the most casual fashion, murmured a few polite words, and would have left if she had not put out her hand to detain him.

It was incredible. Men did not treat her in this way. Men were not bored in her presence, as this Damala obviously was.

"Do you like Paris, Monsieur?"

"Not particularly." He was fidgeting with a sculptured Dresden doll on the table by his side. He put it down carelessly so that it almost fell. Then he began absent-mindedly pulling the petals off a rose which also stood in a vase on the table. "I'm off to Saint Petersburg soon. I'm being transferred there, but I don't imagine I will care any more about Russia than I do about Paris."

"What a strange coincidence," she said. "I've been invited to appear at a Saint Petersburg theater. I was even now debating whether I should go."

He raised an eyebrow but with no real enthusiasm. "Really? You are fortunate, being an actress. The stage is the one and only thing that might possibly interest me." He got to his feet and bowed to her. Quite rudely he turned his back and strode away.

Left alone, she was first infuriated, then amused, then interested. If he had been anyone else she would have considered him just a boor, but Jacques Damala had dark olive skin, black curls, and the brooding face of a fallen angel. Even his rudeness piqued her interest.

He had called her an actress, just as if she were any performer, not Sarah Bernhardt.

She saw him again at an art exhibition. She thought it was an accidental meeting.

The next thing that happened was that she startled her friends by announcing she was going to Saint Petersburg on tour.

The welcome she received in Saint Petersburg was never matched by the fervor of any other city. The frenzy over her amounted to hysteria. In front of her hotel, in front of her theater, everywhere she went, a red carpet was unrolled that her feet might never be touched by the snow. The tsar and his court came to see her and showered lavish gifts on her. All of Saint Petersburg's fashionable world competed to have Sarah as a guest in their homes.

144

The applause after each performance was prolonged until it was brutally hard on her. She was idolized and worshiped not only by the wealthy and the fashionable, but by the people. The horses of her carriage were taken out and the cheering, shouting Russians harnessed themselves to pull her through the streets. She was adored as much for her strange beauty as for her acting.

Indeed, she was more beautiful than ever. Maturity had ripened the loveliness of both figure and face.

All this Jacques Damala saw. He shrewdly realized that the time had come for him to abandon his pose of indifference. Here in Saint Petersburg he was nothing and Sarah was everything. If he did not act quickly she might find another interest. He arranged another "accidental" meeting and he allowed Sarah to put herself out to attract him; then he pretended to be caught by her and in love with her.

As for Sarah, her feelings were real. She was in love, completely and madly. Just as he had hoped, she persuaded him to give up his diplomatic work and return with her to Paris where, she promised him, he would go on the stage with her reputation to push him.

They were married April 4, 1882.

He had confidently expected her to give him the male lead opposite her in *Fédora*, which was going into rehearsals immediately. But much as she was in love, Sarah had too much respect for Sardou. The author was a young man and this play meant a great deal to him. She knew enough of authorship to realize how much of his heart had gone into it. She would not endanger it by giving Damala the leading male role.

Instead, she hired the Ambigu Théâtre on a long-term contract, hired a company, found a play in which there was not too difficult a part for a novice actor, and turned the play and Damala over to a director to handle.

Soon afterwards, Marie Lloyd came one morning to call upon Madame Guerard, knowing that both Sarah and Damala were at rehearsals. She found Madame sitting, dry-eyed but anguished, in the morning room where she was making a feeble pretense at straightening out some household bills.

"Why did she marry him? Why?" Marie burst out without preamble.

"I don't know." Madame's lips began to tremble. "My poor darling. She's bewitched, blinded by this infatuation. Marie, he had not been in this house one hour before he gave me a letter to another woman. He was insolent about it because he knew I would not tell Sarah. I would not hurt her. And the money he is spending on himself—her money!"

"She could have had almost anyone she wished to marry and she chooses a corrupt, debased man like Jacques Damala." Marie twisted her hands in her muff. "Hasn't she heard the stories about him?"

"No, she knows nothing. Or if she hears stories, she says they are nothing but scandalous lies. Maurice is probably the one person she would listen to, but he loves her too much to say anything. Poor Maurice hates him, but he tries not to show it."

Marie sighed. "Well, this is Paris' chance to laugh at Sarah Bernhardt. But no one will. They look at her radiant face and wonder how soon she will be suffering and hurt. I went to the Ambigu on my way here this morning and I watched Damala. The play is a good one and I think he could act if he weren't so arrogant. But he won't listen to the director. He'll play the scenes his way or not at all."

Sarah was radiant. For this brief while she was sublimely happy; when he was in her company Damala was everything a gallant husband should be. She imagined a perfect life for them, saw him as a perfect father to Maurice, and was sure he would prove himself an excellent actor.

This happiness of hers, this glow of being in love, gave her performance in *Fédora* an enriched quality. When she came out on the stage as the Russian princess in her brilliant, exotic robes and gowns with a jeweled tiara on her golden head, she was so beautiful that murmurs of admiration swept through the audience. There were powerful love scenes in the play and she played them with a new intensity of emotion. *Fédora* was a complete triumph for her.

This was her first play in Paris in almost three years and from the first night it was proof that her art had not suffered from her American tour but had gained from it. The scenes were vivid and full of dash and color. The lines Sardou had written were exactly right for her, building to a high pitch of excitement that only she could carry off with success. The Parisian audience besieged the Vaudeville Théâtre for tickets; the play would have a long and solid run.

But at the Ambigu it was disaster. In spite of all that the other actors could do to save the play, Damala's acting was so poor that it was an embarrassing failure. Not even his handsome looks could save him from the scourge and whips of the critic's reviews.

He was furious and blamed Sarah. If she had let him play the male lead in *Fédora* all would have been well. She was just jealous of him and had stuck him in a stupid play so she would not suffer by comparison with him in the same play. He sulked. He was abusive. He would be gone for days and nights and if she wanted to know where he was he told her it was none of her business.

One night there was a violent scene. "I married you only because I thought you could help me on the stage. Did you think I loved you? The more fool you. Now you can do nothing for me, I find. I have no further use for you. There are other women with more money than you have."

"You don't mean what you are saying," she told him, hardly able to say the words.

"Don't I?" He whirled out and slammed the door.

He'll be back, she prayed to herself. He must come back. I love him. He doesn't mean what he said—he's just terribly hurt and disappointed.

Like a sleepwalker she went through her days. When the time came each night for her performance she seemed to rouse herself, throw herself savagely and completely into her part, giving it every ounce of emotion she could so that at night she would be too exhausted to think or to dream. She sank into sleep as if it were death.

Damala's going unloosed a horde of problems with which she had to cope. She had rented the Ambigu Théâtre for him on a long-term contract; she had to pay the rent. The only thing to do

147

was to hastily throw other plays into it to try to get some of her money back. Young as he was, she put Maurice in as manager of the theater.

He was too young. The plays they chose together were not carefully considered; the companies were inexperienced. By the end of May, 1883, the theater had cost Sarah Bernhardt four hundred and seventy thousand francs. She and Maurice realized their mistake and he withdrew as manager and hired another man, Auguste Simon, to save what he could for her.

Not once, in the midst of all these crushing problems and heartache, did she give a poor performance of *Fédora*.

Gradually, so perfect was the front she put up, so excellent was her acting, that all her friends, the public—even Maurice and Madame Guerard—came to believe that the storm of Jacques Damala had passed over Sarah's head without causing her any scars and very little hurt. She was all right again, they told themselves.

It would have shocked them to see her when she was alone at night in her sitting room, pacing the floor, wringing her hands, wondering where he was and what he was doing.

One evening he came back.

"He's in there." Madame Guerard was trembling. She had waited for Sarah to come home from her performance. "He's in there, in his room, behaving as if he had never gone away. What will you do?"

"I will see him, of course." Not even to this dear friend could Sarah let down her pride and show with what eagerness and with what fear she faced this moment of seeing her husband. The torture of the past months was nearly over. He had come back.

She went into the room that had been Damala's. He was lying down on a couch, calmly reading a newspaper, and did not look up as she entered.

She knew this as an old trick of his, pretending indifference. But this time, strangely, it did not attract her. It hurt and angered her. Also, it gave her a moment to examine him without his looking at her. She saw with a shock that his good looks were already beginning to blur with the excess of his dissolute life.

Was it true then, she wondered, these whispers about him?

At that moment he looked up without smiling.

"What are you doing here?" she asked. "Why have you come back after all these months?"

"I need money," he said with callous brutality.

If he had slapped her it would not have hurt so much. He meant it. He did not love her; he had never loved her. Those other things he had said, about using her to get on the stage, they had not been just angry and meaningless words—they were the truth.

"Get out of my house."

He was astounded. She had always pleaded with him before. But he rallied and sneered at her. "It is my house too. I'm sure you never went to the trouble of declaring our separation legal, therefore before the law you are still my wife and I am still entitled to live here. And I know you won't cause any scandal by calling the police to put me out."

She must not give way to tears, she thought to herself. She steeled her face to show nothing.

"Very well. But stay out of my way. Stay out of Maurice's way. We will ignore you as if you were not here."

She told her son and Madame Guerard and the household servants to act as if Monsieur Damala were not in the house. Sarah knew her husband well: he could not tolerate this kind of treatment. In a few days he had gone. She had hardly seen him and did not even know when he left.

Then she said to Maurice, "I'm tired from the long strain of *Fédora*. I am going to take a little vacation all by myself. There is a place I know—Belle Isle. No one will know where I am and I can be quiet and rest. Don't worry if you don't hear from me for a while."

Sarah Bernhardt had never acted so well as then, when she was able to leave Maurice smiling and happy and sure that his mother was completely recovered from her unhappy marriage.

He could not see her in the train going to Belle Isle, her hands clenched, her lips soundlessly repeating, "A fool! I've wrecked my life. How could I have been such a blind, insane, reckless fool?"

{ 15 }

Belle Isle was a lonely place. There were the ruins of an old fort on it, otherwise there was nothing but one whitewashed cottage. Here Sarah was to stay, with an elderly woman to cook her meals for her. Sarah arrived late one night and went immediately to bed. The next morning she awoke wondering where she was.

It was strange not to hear the Paris noises: the sound of wheels on cobblestones, the cries of the flower sellers, the bustle and movement of people in the streets, the whispers of the maids outside her door, Maurice's young voice calling in the hallways.

Here there was silence and peace. There was only the soft clucking of hens in the barnyard. The sighing of wind in the trees. The soft padding of the old woman's felt slippers as she brought Sarah's breakfast. The quiet, *"Bon jour, Mademoiselle,"* as she put rolls and butter down on the table, and then nothing at all but the soundless floating of a bird outside the cottage windows.

Sarah found herself moving slowly. She felt as if she had to: as if her body were a frail shell or that she were ill and needed to walk carefully or she might break.

After her meal she took her easel and her paints to the hillside. She would try to sketch a little of the old wall of the fort.

But no sooner had she begun to make the first strokes than all the thoughts she had been holding back came rushing forth. Damala. His face, under his fur cap in Saint Petersburg, laughing, looking at her with eyes that said he loved her. Damala, shouting at her, "Did you think I loved you? The more fool you!"

She threw herself onto the grass and cried with abandon, as she had not cried for many years. When the storm of tears were over she lay still, looking up at the sky. She was soul-sick. Even the effort to sit up or to move her hand was too much; she lay inert, almost lifeless.

For so many years she had built a decent and honorable life, one that all men and women would respect. She had labored to give her son a good home. She had kept her head high with pride. Now one touch of Damala had soiled her.

If she could have blamed him . . . But she had only herself to blame. It was her own folly, her reckless, foolish desire to take up the challenge which his calculated indifference had posed to her. He had played on her weakness, but it was *her* weakness. She had risked her happiness and the happiness of those dearest to her just because it had seemed impossible that Damala would marry her and she had been that determined he would.

Worse than that, she had fallen in love with him, so completely that even though she now saw him for what he was she was still not cured of it.

At least she had averted an open scandal. By the strict watch she had kept on her own tongue and by the way she had behaved, people were already beginning to forget about him. They thought he had passed through her life like a flash of lightning and that it was all over. Maurice was not hurt; he was happy again.

But what could she do with a nature such as hers which drove her to dare anything, try anything, without ever counting the cost beforehand? Could she be careful in the future?

Just thinking about the future made her feel helpless. She knew she had to go back to work and to the theater and Paris and all the problems of a new play and decide what she must do about the Ambigu Théâtre—but at this moment, lying sprawled ungracefully on the ground of Belle Isle, it seemed impossible. She had no strength any more. She desired nothing—except, perhaps, peace of mind.

Suddenly she felt something wet and cold and soft against her hand. Sarah turned her head and saw a little goat, hardly more than a lamb, whose jet-black nose was investigating her outflung hand. When he saw her move he jumped back a few feet, his own little legs spraddled and his head on one side, watching her.

"Don't be afraid, little one. I won't hurt you," she said softly.

He came closer, sniffed delicately at her hand once more, decided she was alarming and went jumping, stiff-legged and baaing, down the hill.

Sarah laughed. It was a feeble little laugh but it made her feel better. Now she noticed a clump of blue flowers nearby and a yellow butterfly hovering almost motionless over them. Some of the healing quiet of Belle Isle reached her; a few more tears slid down her face but they were soothing ones and soon she slept, more quietly and restfully than she had slept in months.

For days afterward she was listless. She was like a convalescent recovering from a dreadful illness. She ate and slept and sketched a little.

But gradually Belle Isle worked its miracle in her. The clean, bracing air, the long hours of sleep, the good food; the soothing sight of the huge rose bush weighted with its soft pinks against the whitewashed walls of the cottage; the loveliness of twilight and evening stars through her latticed windows; the practical, everyday conversations with the farmwife about the hens and the goats and the stubborn old pig who was always getting out of his pen—all these began slowly to bring her health of body and soul.

One day she realized that she was well again. It was the day when she had gone to fetch the goats home from their hillside and then had had to help chase the pig back into his sty. She found herself running and laughing, racing over the rocks like a young girl.

Suddenly she was brimming over again with energy.

Sardou was anxious for her to open immediately in his new play *Théodora*. It would be a drama of Byzantine courts, intrigues, gorgeous scenery, and costumes. Sarah wanted to play it, but not just now.

I'll do *Froufrou*, she thought. Paris has never seen me in *Froufrou* and it's just the kind of a part I want now. A young girl. Monsieur Sarcey told me that people are beginning to think I must choose older parts, now that I am past forty. *Froufrou* can be my answer to them. It will be taking a chance—and I know I just promised myself to be more careful about taking chances in the future—but I want to show them I'm not ready for the rocking chair just yet.

Before she left Belle Isle she made arrangements to buy it—fort, cottage, hillside, and all.

Sarah Bernhardt might want to change; she would make promises to herself. But it was not in her nature to be anything but reckless and unafraid. At a time when she had lost a fortune at the Ambigu Théâtre, when she was heavily in debt, she bought half an island.

Madame Guerard and Maurice were overjoyed at the glowing, happy face with which she greeted them. The management of the Porte St. Martin Théâtre had left urgent messages asking her to set a convenient time for them to call and discuss *Théodora*.

They were astounded when she announced she would do *Froufrou* instead.

Once again she was instinctively right about herself and the role she needed and could best play at a given moment. The play was a sensational success. The critics claimed they were running out of superlative adjectives to describe her and they could only fall back on the old ones and call her wonderful, divine, glorious.

Young boys and young men came to see her performance and fell in love with her. They wrote her notes saying they wanted to marry her. When their mothers and fathers pointed out that their idol was a woman of forty, they simply refused to believe it. How could they, when she was so young and adorable on stage?

These notes were a tonic for Sarah. It wasn't that she was vain. They proved to her that her art was ageless, that Jacques Damala had not damaged this precious gift of hers, that she still had great stores of untapped talent.

After *Froufrou* she went on to produce and take the leading role in *Théodora*. The character of Théodora was quite the opposite of the charming little Froufrou. Sarah once again was a proud queen, helplessly caught up in intrigues and plots and her own weaknesses. At the end nothing but her own death can save both the king and the man she loves.

Actually, it was not a very good or believable story, yet because

153

of her acting many critics always thought *Théodora* was her best role.

Each year it was whispered that Sarah Bernhardt was about to retire or that Sarah Bernhardt would be changing the kind of parts she played and begin to think only of older women; each year she triumphed anew in her favorite plays and astounded the public with the new ones she created.

"She is incredible!" exclaimed other actors who had reached their prime and were now recognizing that age had put its limitations on them.

"She must have some secret of eternal youth and beauty." Superstitious people nodded their heads and whispered of doctors who probably gave her secret philters and performed strange operations on her to give her youth.

"She is a genius," said others. And truly this seemed the best and only explanation for a Sarah Bernhardt who, at forty, could play Froufrou; at forty-three be a magnificent Tosca; at forty-six take the roles both of Jeanne d'Arc and of Cléopatra; at fifty, try a new kind of role for her, that of a modern, middle-class Frenchwoman in Alexandre Dumas' *La Femme du Claude;* at fifty-two accept the challenge of creating the role of the complex, neurotic character of Lorenzo de' Medici in Alfred de Musset's *Lorenzaccio.*

Of Sarah in *Lorenzaccio*, the critic Jules de Tillet wrote, "This time her triumph was unbounded and unreserved. She went beyond the limits of her art. She gave life to the character of Lorenzo, whom nobody had dared to approach before her. . . . She reached the sublime."

Was she the best actress in the world?

In Italy was Eleonora Duse. Long and violent were the arguments that raged among the partisans of Duse and Bernhardt over which one of them was the reigning queen of the stage. Such discussions only amazed Sarah. Duse was Duse and Bernhardt was Bernhardt; they were nothing alike in style. Wasn't there room in the world for the two of them?

When Eleonora Duse came to Paris once on a tour Sarah was shocked and dismayed to find that, instead of playing the roles that had made the Italian actress so famous, she was going to act in the very plays that were identified with Sarah's name. Surely Eleonora herself would not have done this; she must have yielded to some very poor advice.

As a result her showing in Paris was poor and she did not receive the applause or the acclaim which she would have had, had she stuck to her own parts. No one sympathized with her more, or worried about her more, than did Sarah.

In 1899, when Sarah was fifty-four, she insisted on doing *Hamlet* just as Shakespeare had written him, instead of the poor, garbled translation she had attempted once before. This time not only was she a success but for the first time the French public saw and understood the true greatness of the English Shakespeare.

In 1900 she was once again a young man on the stage: in *L'Aiglon* she was the handsome Duc de Reichstadt.

When Edmond Rostand wrote *L'Aiglon* he was already famous for his great *Cyrano de Bergerac*. His friends protested that he was endangering his writing career by asking Sarah to play the role of the young duke. After all, she was fifty-six years old. But he insisted. Sarah had been the one to introduce one of his very earliest plays, a minor one, to the Paris public when he was still unknown. He was grateful to her, but more than that: he had faith in her. He was convinced that she could do justice to the role.

She did better than that. So wonderfully did she become the duke that, to many people, *L'Aiglon* and the name of Bernhardt were synonymous. Once again every young person in her audience believed for the moment that she was no more than twenty; older people found themselves figuring her age on paper in order to believe it was really possible.

She went on playing *L'Aiglon*, a stripling youth, *until she was sixty-nine years old.*

Offstage she boasted of her years instead of trying to hide them.

Sarah was forty-four when Maurice told her that he had fallen in love and wanted to marry. At first she was upset: she did not want to share Maurice. And it was one thing to have this tall, handsome young man as her escort to parties and see people's eyes widen as they exclaimed, "He's not your son! *Surely* not—your brother perhaps?" It was quite another thing to become a mother-in-law, to lose her escort, to lose her son's heart to another woman.

But when she saw the dark-haired Terka she stopped worrying. The pretty, shy Polish girl adored Maurice and worshiped Sarah. Terka would never separate mother and son.

"But luckily for me," Sarah told her as they sat in the garden planning the wedding, "you aren't an actress, Terka. I can share Maurice with you but not a spotlight. Two actresses in one household would be one too many. We'd probably quarrel and I'm not famous for having a sweet disposition."

They laughed together.

Madame Guerard, watching them, her fingers busy sewing fine, small stitches into Terka's wedding veil, thought that Sarah laughed a great deal more than she used to. Sarah had told her of the funny little lamb on the hillside of Belle Isle and how she had laughed and then had come the healing tears and the peace of mind. Now, more and more, Sarah tried to laugh at her problems instead of fighting them head-on as she had once done.

The wedding was a small one because Terka was too shy to face a huge social gathering. Only the family and a few friends were there.

When it was over Terka and Maurice moved for a while to an apartment of their own, but soon they were back in Sarah's house. There was plenty of room for all of them and Sarah was lonely without them. From then on they lived together except for short periods while Sarah was away on tour or if business called Maurice out of Paris.

It was a happy household. When Terka gave birth to a little girl, Simone, in 1889, there was no prouder grandmother than Sarah Bernhardt, now forty-five years old. Seven years later another grandchild, another girl, was born—Lysiane.

Sarah was not a "grandmotherly" person. It was not in her nature to fuss over infants or bounce them on her knee, even if her busy life had permitted her the time. But for Simone and Lysiane, just as it had once been for Maurice, the sound of her voice was like magic. No matter what they were doing they would drop it the instant they heard the front door open and Sarah's voice calling, "Where are they? Where are my two rascals?"

Simone would run and Lysiane would toddle as quickly as she could, just to be near the warm, vibrant personality of their grandmother, who seemed to have a knack of making everything she said or did so much more exciting than anyone else.

Yet they were well behaved with her. There was no punishment so terrible as having their mother say, "Come, now, off to your rooms. You are being too noisy and you are tiring 'Great.'"

Simone had had trouble with "Grandmother" and the best she could do was something that sounded like "Great." So "Great" became Sarah's name and gradually even Maurice and Terka began to use it.

"Where have you been, Great?" Simone would ask, crouching on her little stool at Sarah's feet and leaning her small head against Sarah's knee.

"I have just come back from America," Sarah would tell her and then go on to describe New York and Boston. "And this time, little one, I went on, out West, to Colorado. And I gave a performance of *La Dame aux Camélias* in a great big tent. A cowboy——"

"What is a cowboy, Great?" Simone asked. Lysiane, too young to understand what was being said, had crawled up onto the arm of Sarah's chair and was leaning against her shoulder, happy just to be near her.

"A cowboy is a man who rides horses all day and takes care of cows—oh, so many cows, Simone. More than you ever saw at one time—thousands! Well, this cowboy lived far away on a ranch but he heard I was coming so he got on his horse and rode one hundred miles just to see the performance; then, when it was all over, he rode another hundred miles back home again. But the reason I happened to know he was there . . ." Sarah broke off to throw head back and laugh. The pins came out of her hair and the rich mass of it tumbled across Lysiane's face, making the little girl crow with delight.

"Why did you know, Great? Tell me, tell me!" Simone begged. She was in a frantic hurry for Sarah to go on with the story.

157

The doorbell was ringing; voices could be heard out in the grand hallways; if Sarah didn't hurry then someone was sure to come in. It was always this way when Great came back from America or England or Sweden or wherever she had been. The house seemed to wake up and people came crowding in and there were flowers everywhere and music and laughing and everyone rushing around so. The little girl wanted Great to herself for these few minutes.

"You see, darling"—Sarah was paying no attention to the voices outside the door. She had the trick of giving her full attention to one person at a time—"you see, in the play there is a man named Armand. He thinks I have done a very bad thing so he gets very angry with me and throws me onto the ground and then throws money in my face. And the cowboy forgot it was just a play and we were just pretending. And he jumped out of his seat and started to rush up the aisle to save me, but people stopped him and we went on playing. Afterward, he came and told me he was sorry but it was so real to him he thought I was being hurt and he was going to punch this Armand in the nose."

She laughed again and Simone laughed. She didn't really understand why the cowboy wanted to punch Armand but it didn't matter; when Great laughed you wanted to laugh too, even if you didn't understand.

The door opened then and several men came in, Maurice with them.

Sarah kissed both the children and told them to run along and she would come up later to the nursery while they had their supper. She must work now. Simone went, but first she whispered to her grandmother, "I'm so glad you are home, Great. You're so beautiful!"

In truth, Sarah at fifty was still beautiful. Her figure had ripened; no longer were there jokes about her thinness. There was no gray in her hair, her skin was still soft and fine. The small wrinkles around her eyes were skillfully hidden by make-up on-stage, but at home she made no effort to conceal them and there was in her face now, not youth, but distinction and character.

She was a businesswoman as well as an actress. Finding that she liked the management of theaters, and that Maurice had a natural bent for this kind of work, she leased first one and then another Paris theater, putting on plays in which she acted when she was in Paris, in which others acted while she was away.

She lost money steadily in these ventures until she discovered the reason: the theaters were too small. So she gambled and bought her own—the large old Théâtre des Nations—which she remodeled and called the Théâtre Sarah Bernhardt. From then on the financial picture improved. This larger theater could hold enough people so that the great successes carried the little failures.

On May 22, 1885, Victor Hugo died.

France's great author had lived a modest man and he wished to die in the same modest fashion. His will read that there were to be no parades and that his coffin was to be placed in a pauper's hearse to be carried to the cemetery.

Whether he wished it or not, the people of Paris loved him far too much to allow him to slip away unnoticed. As the funeral carriage made its way down the Paris streets, the crowds had already gathered. The people were silent except for their tears, but they were there, jamming every inch of space on the pavement. And as the carriage passed, the people left the sidewalks and filled the streets to walk in procession behind him.

Sarah, too, had wanted to pay her great and revered friend this last homage. Cloaked and hooded, she had joined the crowd and was walking among them as silent as they and as anonymous as any of the other Parisians.

But the hood slipped a little and her famous tawny-gold hair was visible. The man walking next to her saw it and recognized her. He nudged the man next to him. "Look!" he whispered.

The other looked and exclaimed, "It's Sarah Bernhardt!"

She had thought she was lost in the crowd. Today she was no different from any of the rest of these grieving Frenchmen. She wanted it that way. She wanted to walk, offering her own weariness and tired feet in slight payment for the wealth of beauty Victor Hugo had brought into her life.

Under her cloak she wore his diamond tear drop around her neck.

But the crowd would not let her play this anonymous part. At first she was unaware of what was happening. A hand would be placed on her arm, pushing her a little; a hand under her elbow to guide her ahead, faster. A space made so that she could walk through and people standing aside and making a passage for her.

The quiet conspiracy parted the crowd like magic. The whisper flew ahead: "Let Sarah Bernhardt move to the front." She was thrust gently but firmly forward until she suddenly found herself in the very front of the procession, walking all alone behind the hearse.

Everyone in Paris knew well the tender bond of sympathy there had been between the author and the actress.

And as the procession marched on through the packed, massed Paris streets, behind the hearse, alone, came the slight figure of Sarah Bernhardt, the tears rolling unashamedly down her cheeks.

The death of Victor Hugo united the French in one single bond of love for a great man. Twelve years later, in 1897, another man was to divide Frenchman against Frenchman, brother against brother, and, in the case of the Bernhardts, mother against son.

This man was an army officer, Captain Dreyfus, a Jew, who had been sentenced to death for supposed treachery to his country and the army. The Dreyfus Affair became a major political issue and *cause célèbre* throughout France. At that time Sarah was rehearsing in a new play by Octave Mirbeau; Mirbeau convinced Sarah of Dreyfus' innocence and asked her to help in the work of freeing him.

At that time only a few people believed Dreyfus to be a victim of a conspiracy and those few were scattered and without organization or a spokesman. Sarah went to Émile Zola, who was a good friend of hers. She told the renowned writer what facts she knew. He became interested and began his own investigation. The results were Zola's famous articles and pamphlets on the case, particularly his *J'accuse!*—"*I Accuse!*"—which cried out for justice, denouncing the real traitors and particularly one Esterhazy, who was guilty of the very treason of which Dreyfus was wrongfully accused.

Because Dreyfus was a Jew and because there were always people who believed the worst about Jews, it had been easy to make him their victim.

Zola was the object of every kind of attack, both honestly mistaken and viciously dishonest. After the publication of *J'accuse!*, a mob stormed his house on January 11, 1898, screaming, "Death to Zola!"

Suddenly a window opened in his house in the rue de Bruxelles and Sarah Bernhardt stepped out onto the balcony, alone. What she tried to say to the crowd was lost in the yell of surprise and outrage that went up at her appearance. Nevertheless, her appearance was so unexpected that the mob halted dead in its tracks. The police closed in, taking advantage of this moment of paralysis to round up the mob leaders and disperse the rest.

But the next day Sarah herself was denounced by those newspapers that were against Dreyfus. Their headlines screamed: SARAH BERNHARDT GOES OVER TO THE JEWS! The articles ranted and raged that since she herself was a Jew, naturally she would be sympathetic to Dreyfus, no matter what his crime.

As much as Sarah believed Dreyfus to be innocent, she also despised the atmosphere of prejudice in which the whole affair was being discussed. She did not consider herself a Jew because one of her grandparents was Jewish, any more than she considered herself Dutch because of another. She was proud of both—but she considered herself wholly French and a Catholic. She took people on individual merit and hated this blind condemnation of any person because of race or religion or nationality.

The violence of public feeling against her was one blow, but a worse one was to follow. She and Maurice had avoided speaking to each other of the case because they knew they held different opinions. Now Maurice could no longer tolerate what his mother was doing; he honestly believed Dreyfus to be a traitor. He took his family away and neither wrote to Sarah nor held any communication with her.

Luckily this period was very brief. Suddenly came the news that one Colonel Henry had committed suicide. There could be only one reason for the suicide of this army officer: his own guilt, for he had produced evidence in support of Esterhazy. Dreyfus was proved innocent!

There were victory celebrations for the freedom of Dreyfus but Sarah did not join in them. She was at home, sorrowing for the wounds this case had cost her beloved France and herself.

She was almost ready to go to bed when she heard the front door of the house open. There was no question of whom it could be. Madame Guerard was already asleep. Only one other person had his own key and could open that door without ringing for a servant. She ran into the front hallway and threw herself into Maurice's arms.

"You've come back!"

"Darling Mama, can you ever forgive me?"

"Forgive you? You had your own convictions; they did not come from prejudice. I would not have respected you if you had pretended to agree with me just because I am your mother." She put her hands on his shoulders and looked lovingly into his handsome face. "Never, never let us mention the Dreyfus case again. It is finished."

Maurice had for years worked with his mother in the management of her theater, in producing her plays and in helping to arrange her tours. He wrote several plays himself which, though not first-rate, did have mild successes, especially when Sarah acted in them. But his chief interest was in theatrical management.

Sarah decided in 1889 to revive *La Dame aux Camélias* once more in Paris. Every time she or her theater needed money, she could always fall back on her stock of a few great plays such as this one, which never failed to bring in the crowds. Maurice agreed and they began to consider the question of the supporting cast for her.

She sent word to him one day that she must see him, privately, in her suite of rooms backstage at the Théâtre Sarah Bernhardt. These five rooms were a third home for her (third, now that she had built a house on Belle Isle). She spent so much time in them that she had furnished them luxuriously: a large drawing room,

162

an outside waiting room, her own dressing room, and a kitchen and dining room downstairs.

It was in the smaller dressing room that Maurice found her waiting for him. At the sight of her face, so pale, so unlike her, at her unusual agitation, he knew that something very serious had upset her. She was dressed as if she had just come in from the street. She was still wearing her hat.

"Something has happened! What is it? Are you ill?" he asked.

"What I have to say to you will be a shock." She turned away from him and went to her dressing table and stood looking down at the cut-glass bottles of perfume and the silver-backed brush and comb. "I do not like to speak of this to you, Maurice, but I must. I have seen Jacques Damala."

At the mention of that name Maurice winced. Were they never to hear the last of him?

She went on. "A friend of mine told me that he was very ill and asking for me. As a matter of fact, Maurice, he is dying. I went to see him. He was living, if you can call it that, in an unspeakable hovel, in the worst of poverty. He was a physical wreck. I said nothing to you then because I knew how you felt about him, but I could not just leave him there to die. I arranged for him to go to a sanitarium."

"That was very kind of you," Maurice said.

"No. He is still my husband. I do not believe in divorce. He has been in the sanitarium for a month and is much improved. Oh, there is no hope for his full recovery. The mark of death is on him; it is only a question of time."

Maurice was moved greatly by pity and love for the difficulty his mother was facing. "I think you did a fine thing. And I am glad you told me about this——"

"Wait. That is not all. That is not why I asked to speak to you privately. This concerns not only our family but *you*, as manager. There is still in Jacques Damala a desire that I can understand. He feels that his life has been a bad one and he has never done anything of which he can be proud. The one good thing in his life was his love of the stage. He doesn't speak of this, but I know —I know what he wants. To act on a stage just once more."

"To act? If he appeared on any stage the audience would boo and hiss him off of it!"

Sarah turned abruptly and faced her son. "Not if he were to act with me."

Maurice fell back into a chair. He stared up at her. "Do you know what you are suggesting? After everything Damala did, you would have him act in a play with you? Hasn't he caused you enough trouble and hurt? You would be creating a scandal out of something almost forgotten."

"Scandal? For myself I don't care. If the tongues wag it means nothing to me. But I would care if it hurt you. You're married and you have your children to think of." She crossed the room and put her gloved hand on her son's shoulder. "He can never hurt anyone again, poor Jacques. If you could see him . . .! And I know that he did care for one thing decently and honestly: he cared for the theater. Perhaps if his family had let him become an actor when he was young he would have been a totally different man."

Maurice was silent but his hand moved up to hold hers. With all his soul he wanted never to hear Damala's name again; he wanted to tell her that she had done more than was humanly generous in sending Damala to a sanitarium. But could he, Maurice, be petty when his mother was being so noble? Could he be small when she was so great?

"If you want him," he forced himself to say, "then we will put him in *La Dame aux Camélias*. And if people talk, you and I will stand together against them. Let them talk. Sarah Bernhardt can do whatever she thinks is right."

When the cast of the show was published in the newspapers and printed on the placards outside the theater and people saw that Jacques Damala was to play Armand to Sarah's Marguerite, it caused a furor of talk and consternation. After all these years, why was Sarah Bernhardt deliberately reviving the humiliation of her marriage? Why give this man the part that hundreds of fine actors were begging for?

The audiences came, curious and inclined to laugh and jeer.

They went away, loving Sarah deeply. They saw her play Marguerite as she had never played her before, so beautifully, so

164

tenderly, that she made up for the pitiful attempts at acting which was all Damala could do. The once-insolent man was now a physical wreck, with only the remnants of his good looks and the tatters of his pride, but Sarah played up to him so deftly that he was able just this once to seem an Armand whom a Marguerite might love.

He was so ill that he had to play many of his scenes sitting down. He was trying, with every ounce of what strength remained in him, to make good in the last chance life would ever offer him. Even when he stumbled over his lines and staggered on his feet, the audiences knew he was trying.

Backstage, before and after the performances, he was quiet, saying little. Only his eyes moved and they followed Sarah with a grateful devotion that brought tears to everyone's eyes.

He died in the last week of November, 1889, very shortly after the play closed.

It was in 1896 that the first official glorification of Sarah Bernhardt took place.

The honor was of a kind that a nation gives very rarely, and then only to one of its most distinguished, most beloved citizens.

"*Sarah Bernhardt Day*—it sounds so grand," Madame Guerard said. She was growing old and feeble now and she looked forward to Sarah's visits to her rooms each day. "Who would have thought, when we were patching and mending that old black dress of yours, when you were at the Odéon, that I would see you so splendid in white satin, setting out for your banquet on Sarah Bernhardt Day?"

"It is a beautiful gown, isn't it?" Sarah turned this way and that to show off the stiff folds of the skirt. "I do wish I knew just what is going to happen today. All I know is that there is to be a banquet. Then the Théâtre de la Renaissance has been sold out for the afternoon and I am to give the second act of *Phèdre* and the fourth act of *Rome Vaincue*. Outside of that I know nothing. Everyone is being most mysterious."

She put her hand over that of her old friend. "I wish you felt well enough to come."

"I will enjoy it every bit as much, hearing you tell me all about it when you come home. Be off now, Sarah, or you'll be late."

When Sarah arrived at the Grand Hôtel in the rue Scribe her carriage had to make its way slowly through the streets jammed with cheering people. And when she entered the banquet hall she found that there were over five hundred guests already seated and waiting for her—all of them the greatest names of France in art, literature, the theater.

She was ushered to her place of honor in the center of the main table. On her right was the French Minister of Fine Arts, on her left was the representative of the president of the Republic.

Dazed, she went through the motions of eating. Over at the long table on her left she could see Mounet Sully and François Coppée; Edmond Rostand waved to her from the far end.

When the banquet meal was out of the way, Victorien Sardou rose to speak. Though there were other and greater writers there, it had been thought appropriate to have Sardou alone speak since his plays had been written solely for Sarah to act in.

Quietly, almost conversationally, he reviewed for the assemblage the history of Sarah Bernhardt and what she had done for the French theater. As he spoke it all came back to her—her days at the Conservatoire, her mishaps at the Comédie Française, her first little successes in *Athalie* and *Le Passant*, Victor Hugo and the diamond tear drop for her Doña Sol in *Hernani*, her return to the Comédie Française and all of the triumphs and heartaches since then.

Someone nudged her. She realized that Sardou had finished speaking and that everyone was applauding him and looking at her. She must somehow get to her feet and answer.

Sarah had no idea then or afterward what she said. That she thanked them, she knew; that she paid tribute to the great teachers and managers and directors and authors who had so helped her, she knew. But how she said it—in what words—she could not remember.

The private celebration of the banquet over, it was time for the public to share in Sarah Bernhardt Day.

She was driven to the Théâtre de la Renaissance. At two-thirty in the afternoon the curtain went up on the second act of *Phèdre* before a house that was packed from gallery to orchestra. When it was finished and the curtain down, she rushed backstages toward her dressing room.

Henri Bauer, a journalist, who had been one of the organizers of this "Day," stopped her.

"Oh Henri, not now! I simply cannot take any bows. I must change for *Rome Vaincue*; the costume of the grandmother takes time to adjust correctly."

"That can wait," he told her. "We have a surprise for you. You have been performing for us and now we are going to perform for you."

He led her back to the stage. The scenery of *Phèdre* had been hastily cleared away. All that remained on the stage, on a low dais, was a great golden throne. To this he led Sarah while the whole audience came slowly and reverently to its feet. When she was seated, François Coppée came forward and read a sonnet in her honor. He was followed by Catulle Mendès, André Theuriet, Edmond Rostand, and Edmond Haraucourt, each with his own poem dedicated to Sarah Bernhardt.

The orchestra played a "Hymn to Sarah Bernhardt," specially composed in her honor.

The audience applauded, but what was most impressive was the dignity and gravity of both those in the audience and those on stage. They were fully conscious of participating in a historic moment.

It was, however, a historic moment that was to be repeated over and over again, with Sarah Bernhardt Days going on year after year and in every country—to the point where Sarah used to groan, "Oh, not again! I can't go through with it again.

{ 16 }

It was the year 1905. Sarah was in Rio de Janeiro, Brazil, after a most successful tour of South America, planning to go on next to the United States. In fact, the tour had been a dazzling one. Her fame was never greater. In one theater in Buenos Aires crowds had almost suffocated her with their enthusiasm. One admirer had tossed costly jewels onto the stage at her feet.

This was her last night. Tomorrow she would take ship for New York. The play was *La Tosca*, which Sardou had dedicated to her and which was to become later on the story for one of Puccini's greatest operas. It was one of Sarah's favorites.

The last scene was extremely dramatic, for she hurls herself over a parapet to her death far below.

It was a dangerous jump. The stagehands had explicit instructions that behind the make-believe walls were to be spread thick mattresses over every inch of space, since Sarah could not be positive that she would jump onto exactly the same spot each time.

This one night someone erred. The back floor was not entirely filled with soft mattresses, or else one of them had been accidentally moved. One corner was bare.

Sarah gave her last, despairing cry and threw herself over the wall. She fell and struck her right knee painfully on the hard bare floor of the stage. She fainted and had to be carried to her dressing room. Within seconds the knee was swollen badly.

She took no bows that night. When she regained consciousness it was to find the theater manager hovering over her with a shocked and horrified face. Her leg was swollen and throbbing, painful to touch.

168

"I have sent for a doctor—but at this time of night, it may take a while," he babbled.

"Never mind the doctor," she said. Sarah had so much careless confidence in the strength of her body that she could not conceive that anything serious had happened. "I just hurt my knee a little. Don't worry about it and don't cause any fuss about it. I must take that ship tomorrow for the United States."

"But you can't!"

The rest of the cast said the same thing. "You can't travel tomorrow.

When the doctor came, he was even more emphatic. "You must stay here and be cared for until that knee is better or I won't answer for the consequences."

"Nonsense!" she told them firmly. "I have my engagements to fill in New York. I simply must be there; the tickets have been sold for the performances and they are expecting me. The schedule cannot be changed. If I miss this boat the next one could not possibly get to New York in time."

In spite of all their protests, she insisted. The next morning she had to be carried to the ship, but she went. Once on board she immediately fainted again.

This time, when she opened her eyes, it was to find a man looking down at her out of a dirty and unshaven face. He scratched at his whiskers and she saw that his fingernails were black with dirt and grime.

"Who are you?" she asked sharply.

"The ship's doctor, Madame. It looks like you're going to be my patient." He got to his feet and shambled to the foot of the bed. He started to lift the sheet. "Now let's take a look at that knee of yours."

She was furious. "You won't take any look at my knee and you won't stay in this room another minute. Do you think I want your dirty hands touching that bandage? Get out of here."

Some of the cast tried to argue with her. "We will be twenty days on board this ship, sailing up the coast before we reach New York. You must have your leg attended to. We asked the

169

captain to insist that the doctor bathe and clean his hands. Please let him come in now and attend to your injury."

"I won't have him near me. I don't trust him. If I just keep the leg quiet and propped up it will be all right. When I was a child I survived a fall worse than this one. I've found that a little rest is all I ever need and I'm as fit as ever."

This time Sarah was wrong.

Those twenty days were disastrous. Without proper medical care the knee became infected; by the time she reached New York and good doctors it was too late. The doctors were able to dress and clean and treat it, but they warned her that serious damage had been done to both nerve and muscle.

The injury grew slowly and steadily worse over the next years. By 1908 she could walk only with the greatest difficulty; by 1911 she always had to lean on someone's arm; by 1913, she could walk only a step at a time before stopping or having to sit down.

Yet all this time the audiences suspected nothing. She went right on playing as if nothing had happened. Some of her most outstanding roles were created in these years: *Adrienne Lecouvreur*, Pelléas in Maeterlinck's *Pelléas et Mélisande*, Prince Charming in Jean Richepin's *La Belle au Bois Dormant*, Lucrece Borgia in the play of that name by Victor Hugo, her role of the Poète in Alfred de Musset's *La Nuit de Mai*.

It took a great deal of thought and careful, skillful placing of chairs and tables, pillars and benches on the stage in whatever play she was acting. Her own courage and talent did the rest. From out in front she seemed to be walking all over the stage. She seemed to be moving as fluidly and as gracefully as ever.

Actually she could only take one step at a time. What no one realized was that she took a step and leaned her hand behind her so that it was not obvious that she could put no weight on her leg. Or she took another step and sat in a chair, as naturally as though it were a part of the regular stage action. Or another step and leaned back against a wall; placed her hand and weight on someone's shoulder. By the movement of her hands or her body she could create the *illusion* that she was in motion even when her feet were still.

But the pain was persistent, ceaseless, and constantly growing worse.

The time finally came, in 1915, when the doctors had to tell her the truth.

"We can operate," one of France's greatest surgeons told her, standing by her bedside after an examination, "but we cannot be assured of success. You must be prepared for the worst. We may have to——" He was having difficulty trying to find the words to soften the blow.

She knew. Her hands tightened convulsively on the sheet, almost tearing it. But her face and voice were calm. "You mean I may lose my leg, is that it?"

"Yes."

He left her. He knew there were no words to help her in her private agony. She did not want Maurice or Simone or Lysiane just now. If only Madame Guerard were with her! But that good soul had died a few years ago, quietly and peacefully, wanting no more fuss over her death than she had caused in her life. But for Sarah there was an aching emptiness. Her oldest and best friend, the one person she could always share pain and heartache with, was gone.

Oh, surely the operation must be a success! This terrible thing could not happen to her.

Her hands clawed at the bedcovers; she twisted until her head was burrowed into the pillow, stifling her moans. It can't happen! Please God, it can't happen!

But it could. She knew it could.

"No, no . . ." She was raging now. The control over her temper that she had so slowly won these past twenty years had snapped again and she was as rebellious as she had been as a child.

Maurice heard her and ran into the bedroom. "Oh Great—Sarah——" He, too, had heard the surgeon's report and was heartbroken.

"Don't stand there looking like that, feeling sorry for me!" she stormed at him.

He was surprised but not hurt. This was the first time in their lives she had ever turned her temper on him, but he knew that her spirit was rousing itself to meet her ordeal—another person might cry and weep but Sarah must storm. Only in that way could she not be defeated.

And Maurice, for the first time, saw that she was old. She had been thin when she was young, then she had matured into a full, ripe beauty. Now she was thin again and wasted and all her suffering of the past ten years, the sleepless nights and the torture of acting while in pain, had left their cruel marks on her face.

"Don't look at me like that! I won't be pitied." She was snapping at him. Her great, huge eyes were burning. Deep in their sockets, they were still more alive, more unquenchable, than any eyes he had ever seen. Her thick mass of hair was almost pure white against the pillow. "I won't let them make a cripple of me."

"Of course not, Great," Maurice soothed her. "We'll find another doctor. I'll get the best surgeons in the world to operate."

Her head fell back on the pillow. The anger drained away. He saw—and could hardly believe—that she was trying to smile.

"No, no, Maurice. I'm an old fool to try to fight what is inevitable. If I hadn't been so stubborn in Rio de Janeiro years ago this wouldn't have happened. The doctor is right." Sarah threw back the covers. "Look at it. Look at that leg. It would be a miracle if they could save it."

Maurice looked and was sickened at what he saw.

"Don't worry any more, my dear," his mother told him. "I shan't make any more fuss. You may tell the surgeon he can operate whenever he is ready and if—well, if the worst comes we'll face it."

The worst came. She underwent the operation, then they were forced to tell her that it was too late and they must amputate her leg above the knee.

"Do it then," she whispered, only her indomitable will alive in her eyes as she looked up at them. "Do it now. Quickly."

After it was all over she was brought to Belle Isle to recuperate.

Ever since that day when she had come here to find strength and refuge after Damala had treated her so cruelly, this was the home she loved the most. She had built a house and then, after Maurice had married and there were grandchildren and all of her friends

172

got into the habit of coming to Belle Isle to spend their vacations with her, she had built and built until there were many guest cottages nearby. There were fragrant gardens everywhere and outdoor terraces where she could sit in the sun.

Here she had come for solace when Madame Guerard had died. Here Maurice had wept in her arms when his sweet, gentle Terka had died just two years before.

Once again the sunshine and peace of Belle Isle were healing Sarah Bernhardt. It was characteristic of her that, once the pain and shock of the operation were over, she wasted not a single moment on bitterness at what fate had done to her. The leg was gone. Very well, she must now learn to live without it.

For the first time in many years she awoke without the dreaded throbbing in her leg. For the first time she could sleep. Health came back to her, and with it her old energy.

The surgeon brought crutches for her. She refused to use them.

"They make me look grotesque, with my shoulders hunched over like that. I have always been noted for my straight back. I won't have people see me like that."

A wooden leg was made for her. She tried it and discarded it.

"It makes me stump and thump about so. I practiced years in the Conservatoire to learn to walk gracefully and I'm not going to change it now."

"But, Madame Bernhardt," the surgeon protested, "what possible difference can it make how you walk now? Or what people think when they see you? As a doctor, I say that it is important for your morale and your health that you learn again to walk, no matter how difficult or how odd you may appear."

"Yes, Great," Maurice joined in with him, "what difference does it make now?"

"What difference——?" Sarah stared at the two men. Then she looked at Simone and Lysiane, both of them young and pretty now.

Simone spoke up: "Of course it makes a difference. No woman wants to look ugly."

"Thank you, my dear," Sarah said, "but even you don't understand. All of you seem to think that because I have lost my leg everything has changed. I am no longer an actress. Believe me, it isn't vanity that makes me talk of my straight back and of what people think of me. Well, let me tell you all now: I am an actress, I am still an actress, I am going on being an actress. One leg or two —I shall act!"

The woman on the bed struggled, refusing their help, until she had pulled herself into a sitting position against her pillows. Around her shoulders was a fine, white silk brocaded jacket. There was color in her cheeks from the sun and from the heat of her argument with them. She looked ten years younger than before her operation. The lines of suffering had disappeared from her face.

"You see? Sitting, I look just the same. When I am sitting I remind no one that my leg is gone. So from now on, I shall always sit!"

Lysiane ran to her grandmother and hugged her. "Oh, I am so glad. I couldn't bear to think of you being changed. And when you are sitting up like that, you *are* the same as you always were."

Sarah ordered a little chair to be made for her. On each side, two wooden shafts, about six feet long, stuck out. They could be folded up, just as the chair could. It was very light, weighing no more than six pounds, and two men, one on each side of her, could carry it anywhere, in and out of carriages or motor cars or trains. As soon as she was settled, the shafts were holded up so that she simply sat in what looked like an ordinary chair with a rather high back.

At night the chair was folded up beside her bed; in the morning it was unfolded for her. She would allow no help in getting out of bed or into her chair but pulled herself upright with the help of her hands and a cane. She could stand erect, using the cane as support, for a considerable length of time; she had had plenty of practice easing the weight off her bad leg onto her good one before the operation.

Still, it was not easy, she had to learn to counterbalance the loss of weight. Sometimes she fell but she would allow no one to help her or pick her up. She forced herself to do it alone.

She had her dressmakers put special stiffening underneath her gown on the right side. That, with the clever use of boned hoops, completely concealed the fact that her right leg was missing. Sarah had no need to hide herself from the waist down with blankets. She could go on wearing beautiful gowns.

When she sat in "her chair" there was no disfigurement visible. Her back was as straight as ever. Her movements were fluid and natural.

But—she had said defiantly—she would act. She *had* to, she needed money badly. But how could she? She was seventy-one years old. She was crippled. No one had any suggestion as to how she would go back on the stage.

Not even Maurice really understood how desperately she wanted to be back at work. The Théâtre Sarah Bernhardt was making money for them, but not enough and he was seriously worried over their huge debts; still, it revolted him to think of his mother sitting in front of an audience again, an audience who had come to stare in curiosity at Sarah Bernhardt with one leg.

Energy was once again pushing her, making her bold. World War I was at that moment raging all over Europe. Sarah, telling no one, wrote to the Minister of Fine Arts and offered her help.

The result of that letter was that Sarah was included in a benefit performance given in Paris to raise money for the soldiers. She recited a poem, seated all through the performance.

She knew that there was intense curiosity in that audience and that eyes were constantly going to her skirt—at first. Then the music and power and loveliness of her voice captured them and they forgot that it was a maimed woman speaking to them and were conscious only of the emotion her voice created in them.

Afterward, backstage, Maurice and Lysiane hugged her, crying. "You were right, Great! You are still an actress," Lysiane told her. And Simone, who had recently married, rushed up to her in excitement.

"I sat out front and watched you and you were superb. There must be scenes or acts from plays that you could put on, Great, just as you did today, reciting poetry. The way you used your hands and your body, it actually seemed as if you were moving."

With this taste of an audience again, Sarah badgered and heckled officials until she was allowed to go to the front to visit the soldiers who were going into battle. To them, too, she recited poetry and did bits of scenes from her famous plays. To the soldiers, knowing of her injury, her courage became their courage and they welcomed her as one of themselves.

For this—and for all the past work she had done to raise the standards of French theater and spread the glories of French art among the nations of the world—Sarah Bernhardt was given the medal of the French Legion of Honor.

She decided to go on tour in America. Maurice helped her select certain dramatic scenes from her best plays, scenes in which she would not have to stand. From a financial point of view the tour was a success, but when she returned to Belle Isle her family was shocked at the bitter despondency in her face.

"I played in vaudeville houses," she told them that first night as they all gathered in Great's room to hear her news, "and I was just another act sandwiched in between the jugglers and the acrobats. Oh, I was applauded. But they came to see me out of curiosity. It was miserable; I wasn't really acting, I was doling out bits and scraps of emotional scenes."

"The newspapers were very complimentary, Mother," Maurice assured her.

She looked at him for a moment with such frustration and unhappiness in her eyes that he could not bear it and turned his face away.

"Don't you understand?" she said. "How much I would just once more love to be in a real play, and go through rehearsals once more, to see words on paper take form and meaning and become life on a stage in a real theater?"

Maurice could not answer her and her head fell back against her chair. She knew what he was thinking: she was almost seventy-five now. She was old and crippled. It was hopeless. She was asking for the impossible.

But, unknown to her, a young playwright named Louis Verneuil was asking himself at that very moment if it *was* impossible. He had worshiped Sarah for years though he had never met her. It seemed to him a terrible waste of genius that Sarah Bernhardt should become a vaudeville act for curiosity-seekers.

He went to Maurice and told him that he was writing a play for his mother.

Maurice was amazed. "Don't you realize that she can't walk?"

"Well, the character won't walk."

Maurice's loving concern for his mother urged him to protest. "She can play an act running for a quarter of an hour. But she could never learn three or four acts and play them for months."

Louis Verneuil explained that the character in his play *Daniel* would not be on stage except for the last two acts of a four-act play, yet she would be a central figure and have a part that would call upon all her dramatic and emotional ability. The play was not yet written—it would be written with both Sarah's talents and limitations in mind.

"Let me try," he begged Maurice.

Unconvinced, Maurice agreed.

By November of 1919 the play was finished and arrangements were made for Verneuil to meet Sarah for the first time and read her the play *Daniel*.

Young as he was, Louis Verneuil was already a successful playwright. He had met all of the great people of France's theater world; he had met Anatole France, the renowned writer; he had been introduced to such world-famous political figures as Clemenceau and Poincaré. Yet none of these affected him as did the slight, frail figure sitting in the armchair in front of her fireplace, dressed in a long, blue wool gown, holding out her still-lovely hands to welcome him.

It was not her past triumphs that made his heart beat faster and his tongue seem tied in knots. It was the vibrant warmth and strength of will and incredible charm that was still in Sarah's face and in her voice.

"You have written a play for me, Monsieur? How very, very kind of you." Then, as she saw that he was still tongue-tied and embarrassed, she asked him to throw a log of wood on the fire, and this simple, homely act broke down the barriers and he could settle himself opposite her, bring out his manuscript, and begin to read the play.

When he had finished he saw to his amazement that she was

crying. She motioned him to come to her. He knelt down and she kissed his forehead, murmuring, "Thank you. Thank you." That was all.

❧{ 17 }❧

All of Paris was stupefied when it was announced to the newspapers that Sarah Bernhardt was returning to the theater to star in the play *Daniel*. Everyone had thought she was finished. People rushed to get tickets—some out of curiosity, some out of loyalty to her as their onetime idol, some because they felt that this might be their last chance to see Sarah on a stage.

It was 1919 and she was seventy-five years old.

Opening night, boxes in the Théâtre Sarah Bernhardt that were only supposed to hold six people had double that number. People sat on the folding chairs in the aisle; they stood all around the sides and at the back of the house in defiance of all fire laws.

The curtain rose.

Onstage a husband and wife spoke of Daniel—poor, unhappy Daniel, who had hidden himself away in his house, ill and lonely. The audience soon learned that Geneviève, the wife, neglected by her husband, was in love with another man. She knew that the husband would soon find her out.

As act followed act, the tension rose. Geneviève was facing ruin, but more than anything else she feared that the vengeance of her husband would fall on the man she loved. There was only one thing to do—appeal to Daniel for help.

Then the curtain rose on the third act. Sarah, as the man Daniel, sat in an armchair, wearing a dressing gown. He was wasted from long years of ill health and his hopeless love for Geneviève. To his shock and amazement, and to the delight of his yearning heart, had come this unlooked-for wonder: Geneviève had come to him. She needed him. She wanted his help.

All of the hopeless passion and longing, the incredible joy of seeing his beloved once more, the futile anger at himself for being ill and weak when she needed a strong protector—all of these things were in Sarah's voice and acting.

The audience was gripped in her spell. How could they have forgotten how wonderful that voice was? How many shades of emotions it could carry in a whisper? How vividly she could create strong feelings by just slightest motion of her hands?

And then Daniel realized that the one thing he could do to help the woman he loved was to pretend to the husband that it was he —not some unknown man—who had taken her away and stolen her love. He realized that he must turn the husband's anger onto himself and at that point Daniel became a figure of tremendous pathos, evoking heartbreaking emotion.

The audience felt it, and when the curtain fell on that scene there was a spontaneous outburst of applause.

It had been planned beforehand, unknown to Sarah, that every one who came to the theater that night would bring her a flower or a bunch of flowers to present at the end of the play. The audience could not wait until then. Caught up by the sheer mastery of her performance, they stopped the show and threw their flowers onto the stage where the curtains had parted to reveal her, sitting still in Daniel's armchair. The floor was covered in a few seconds; soon the flowers were piled as high as her arms. Still they came, the soft blossoms pelting through the air from gallery and boxes, to the accompaniment of "Bravo's!" from all parts of the house.

When the demonstration was over, she was shoulder-high in flowers. They covered the stage and her chair. Afterward, back-stage, the stagehands found them piled as high as a haystack.

The audience cried and Sarah cried. She was back once more where she belonged. This tribute to her had not been a kind gesture to a queen who had abdicated but to one who still reigned.

Emboldened by this success, she decided to do something that had been long in her mind: to play the part of Athalie, Racine's great tragic heroine. She had wanted to do the role ever since she had appeared in the play as the young boy. Zachariah, over fifty years ago.

"But how can you?" Maurice objected. "Athalie walks into the Temple of the Lord—not once but twice. She storms in the last time."

They were at Belle Isle, sitting together on the wide porch. Sarah leaned forward, letting her scarf slip to the porch floor. "I know that is how it has always been played. But I have been doing a lot of research, and in the days of the Old Testament a queen did *not* walk in public. She was always carried on a litter by slaves or, as in Athalie's case, by soldiers. A queen in those times must always look down on the people and it would be considered undignified of her to walk."

"But——"

"No, think it over. Don't give me an answer now. It is a risk for our theater and for you, so you must help me decide. Right now it is time for dinner. Will you wheel me in?"

Maurice was delighted to see the animation and sparkle return to his mother's face since the production of *Daniel.* He knew he had been wrong to try to shield and protect her. It thrilled him to see her once more excited about life and people. Belle Isle was once more becoming the mecca of all her friends' lives— her old friends and new ones, too. Young playwrights came to see her; actors and actresses sought her advice.

This morning for example, there had been just herself and Maurice and Lysiane and Louis Verneuil in the house. Louis was in love with Lysiane and courting her. But now there were twenty people for dinner, both invited and unexpected guests.

The conversation that night was about a play of George Bernard Shaw.

"I admire him tremendously," Sarah stated vigorously, "but my style of acting would never suit either his plays nor Mr. Ibsen's. They represent a new school of the theater and an excellent one."

"We called our kind of plays and acting the 'natural' kind of drama," an older playwright remarked. "That was because Molière introduced something much more natural than the artificial sort of thing that had been done before him; but actually 'romantic'

180

would be the better description of us. We are unnatural compared to the new kind of play Mr. Ibsen writes."

Sarah looked first down the whole length of the long table to be sure that everyone was being served with *glacé* and fresh strawberries and little cakes before she spoke. "It was dear Victor Hugo who began our romantic kind of plays. Thunder and lightning, intrigues, duels at dawn, ridiculous codes of honor that kept the hero from marrying the heroine, usually death for the lovers in the end—but still it was a new thing to the theater. For the first time our plays were honest. They dealt with subjects that had been forbidden before—love and hate, infidelity, passions. We weren't afraid of anything."

When dinner was over and the long evening of good talk, laughter, and games had ended, Sarah settled herself on her couch in her bedroom before the open windows. All the rest of the house was quiet and asleep. She never had felt more wide-awake.

Athalie. Did she dare try it? The problem of age, here, was no problem at all. Athalie, that most wicked and evil of Racine's heroines, was not young but she was a woman of fire and fury, of malevolent wickedness. Sarah was sensible. She knew that her body was old and frail. Did she still have the passion, the spirit, to do justice to a character like Athalie?

Sarah had been wanting to play Athalie for so long, and had studied her so carefully, that she felt that she knew this tyrant queen as well as she knew herself.

I can do it!

Without realizing it, Sarah had grasped her cane and struck the window casement with it, in her determination. In the next room, Maurice—watchful as he always was now of his mother's health—awoke immediately. He put on a dressing gown and came hurrying in to her.

"What is it? Are you all right?"

"Oh yes. I was just arguing with myself about Athalie. Maurice, I know I can play that part.

He rubbed his eyes sleepily. "Of course you can. I never had any doubt of it, really. I just wasn't sure that you should put yourself through that kind of ordeal. But if you want to play Athalie, I'll begin gathering the cast immediately."

"Dear Maurice." She hugged him.

And when he was gone, sleep was farther away from her than ever. Her mind was racing. If she were to play Athalie, it would be her intelligence that would have to create the part; she no longer had that superb vitality of youth to create emotions by sheer force of personality. She must think.

She smiled to herself and pulled her warm, fleecy robe tighter around her shoulders as the night chill came in through the open windows. She was grateful to Louis Verneuil for having given her the chance, in *Daniel*, to come back to her place as an actress in the theater, but *Daniel* was a mediocre play. *Athalie* was a great French classic.

When people argued, as they did for many years, which role of Sarah Bernhardt's was the greatest—her Phèdre, her Marguerite, her Fédora, her L'Aiglon—only a few perhaps would have chosen her Athalie.

Yet in many ways it was her greatest role because it was the ultimate triumph of her talent, her skill, and her intelligence over age and sickness and her frail, maimed body. The fire of her genius had burned down to ashes. It was a miracle of that genius that this last burst of flame should have burned so high, so brilliantly, so flawlessly.

She was seventy-six years old when the curtain rose on that historic performance of *Athalie*. This time there was no question that the audience had come out of curiosity and loyalty to her. Nothing much was expected, but it would have been discourteous for critics or audience to stay away.

Athalie did not appear until the second act. The audience settled down to watch the excellent performance of the actors who took the roles of the High Priest and his wife and Zachariah, as they discussed the dangerous situation confronting them. Athalie was menacing the Temple: she had permitted them to go on existing, but the people were forbidden to worship there. Now she was threatening to pull down the Temple itself.

Then came the rise of the second-act curtain. Zachariah came running onstage to inform his mother that the Temple was even at that moment being profaned by the appearance in it of Athalie herself.

The curtain dropped on that scene, rose immediately for the next.

Athalie, seated on her gorgeously draped litter, was being carried by her slaves into the chaste simplicity of the Temple rooms. She gazed about with the strange fascination of one who had come to a forbidden place; there was triumph in her gaze, and fear as well. The slaves stood motionless while she looked about.

Her attendant, Hagar, spoke:

> "Madam, why stay in such a place as this,
> Where every sight offends and wounds thine eye?"

Then Athalie spoke. The startled critics looked up from their little notebooks forgetting to jot down their comments. They had expected one kind of voice, but this was a different Athalie. This new voice was low and thin, without heat or fire. The audience stirred, not sure whether they liked it. All the other Athalies had played the scene in an irritated, angry manner. But Sarah was playing it as Racine had written it—"vexed and *weak*"—a woman troubled with superstition and fear.

And when her other attendants and her High Priest continued to beg her to leave, Athalie paid no heed but said:

> "Both of you lend me an attentive ear.
> I do not wish now to recall the past,
> Nor give account to you for blood I shed.
> A sense of duty prompted all my acts."

"Oh, clever Sarah," murmured one newspaper critic to his friend, "she's playing this with the emphasis on Athalie's troubled conscience. *Very* clever of Sarah indeed! That kind of Athalie won't take any strength to play."

The audience, too, was fully alert and listening and watching, fascinated. They were being presented with an Athalie who was intelligent as well as wicked, aware of her crimes, proud of having committed them, yet afraid before this unknown God, nerving herself to overcome her fear because somehow the menace of the boy in her dreams must be met and challenged.

Then she saw him—the young boy, the foundling of the Temple. He was the boy in her dreams!

The entire audience felt a strange chill run up their spines. Athalie's face was startled, then intent—horribly so. Then it changed. All the cunning and the trickery that Jezebel, her mother, had taught her came to the fore. Her face became sweet and motherly, enchanting in its softness. Only the glitter of her evil eyes gave her away.

Other actresses had been regally imperial or cross in dealing with the boy. Or some actresses, playing Athalie, had shown their fear of him.

But Sarah's Athalie was a temptress. Her words caressed him; she purred at him, was tender and playful with him as she painted for him a lovely picture of what life in her palace would be like if only he would leave this Temple and come with her.

Caught up in the snare of her voice, the audience was pleading in their hearts for the boy to stand firm, not to listen to her, to realize that there was murder in her heart. That voice of Sarah's was still so magnificently a musical instrument, so bewitching, that it seemed to them it could have charmed any innocent boy.

A friend nudged the critic. "What do you think of that?" he whispered.

"*Mon Dieu!*" said the other, groping for his handkerchief to wipe his forehead.

Then came the fifth act, the last act, when Athalie returned to the Temple of God. This time she came as a warrior Queen in her litter, borne on the backs of her armed soldiers.

She had conquered her fear and her superstition. She was ruthless. She had come to destroy both the boy and the Temple, but she was too late. The High Priest was ready for her. Already he had sent word to the people in the city that their true king lived. Already the armed bands of the Levites were waiting in the Temple to surround Athalie.

Trapped, defeated, Athalie was a tiger. She said little, but her words rang with fury and hatred and venom.

"I'm wrong. I'm wrong," muttered the critic, on the edge of his seat with excitement. "Sarah did not play the role that way because of any weakness. Where does she get that force and strength?"

It was not so much what she said. This scene, the climax of the play, showed Athalie as fiery, proud, disdainful. Brought to bay by her enemies but hating them, she defied them with every line of her body and every snarling motion of hands and face. The last words were the High Priest's as he ordered her taken from the Temple to face certain death at the hands of the people—yet all attention was on the now-silent Athalie. Her glittering eyes said more than words. Defeated, she was still the most challenging, impressive figure on the stage as slowly her soldiers carried her off to her doom.

The final curtain fell.

Hidden from the audience, the cast waited, motionless, in their places. Sarah still sat in her litter, waiting. And the silence grew until it seemed to be mocking her and the thought, the dreaded thought, of failure gripped her so that her hands clenched and unclenched.

Then it came: wave after wave of applause, resounding and billowing and thundering through the curtain. The actors who played her warriors picked up the litter, the cast stood still in their places, and the curtain rose.

After the ovation, though the applause was still going on, Sarah motioned for the curtains to close and for herself to be carried off the stage.

Maurice came over to her. "They're still calling for you, Great. You have to go back."

"Nonsense. Let the rest of the cast take the bows. I'm tired and I'm an old woman. I'm not going back there."

But Maurice noticed that she did not move from her Queen's litter, even though her folding chair was brought. He noticed, too, that she was listening with excitement—though she tried not to show it—to the rising storm of handclaps and cries of "Bravo!" and "Sarah!" which were increasing from the audience.

What's she up to, now? he thought fondly.

He did not know that she was remembering Henry Abbey and it was as if he were talking to her: *Don't go out there yet, Sarah. You've done something extra-special tonight. Let 'em wait. Let 'em want you so badly they'll tear the house down to see you.*

And it wasn't until it really seemed as if the excited crowd was going to do just that, tear down the house, that she motioned for her litter to be picked up and carried on stage. The noise of applause then rocked the theater. She faced them like the showman she was, regally bowing her head, spreading her arms in a loving gesture of thanks which seemed to envelope everyone. The audience responded with a renewed fever of clapping from hands that were sore and wrists tired; they shouted her name with throats that ached.

"Sarah! Bravo!! Sarah!"

They would not let her go nor let the curtain close until Maurice became seriously concerned for her strength. Coming out onto the stage, he held up his hands for silence. Gradually the house quieted and with simple, quiet dignity Sarah spoke, thanking them for their applause in the name of the cast and herself.

Then the curtain closed.

The audience filed slowly out into the lobby of the theater, still speaking in amazement and excitement of what they had seen. Georges Clairin, Sarah's old friend, happened to be walking behind the critic and his friend.

"That was the best Athalie I ever saw," the friend said.

"I wonder." The critic considered it thoughtfully. "Perhaps not the best. I'm not sure but that I don't prefer Madame Segond-Weber's Athalie, but certainly Sarah Bernhardt's was the most intelligent portrayal I have ever seen."

Georges Clairin's heart rejoiced. They were not speaking of Sarah in the exaggerated terms they might have used for a legendary character, nor with condescension for a has-been actress. Sarah to them was a "working" actress, someone to be compared and judged.

The critic adjusted his cloak. "Did you notice how few gestures she used? I always thought—and Sarcey said the same to me, before he died—that Mademoiselle Bernhardt used too many gestures. Do you remember that scene, when she played Hermione and sat tearing off the petals of an oleander bush? In *Andromaque*? It was the sort of thing her audiences liked, but I always thought it unnecessary. Tonight she made not one motion that didn't have meaning to it."

His friend nodded. "I still think this was the best *Athalie*. I wonder what she will do next?"

Georges Clairin felt tears sting his eyes. What would she do next? In the eyes of everyone she was not only the Divine Sarah, but after tonight she seemed indestructible. But he knew better. He saw her often and he knew that her spirit and will could not keep life much longer in that poor body.

She had another moment of great personal happiness—this time it was the wedding of her granddaughter Lysiane to Louis Verneuil. From the first day they met, when he brought her the play *Daniel* to read, she had loved him as a second son. On the day of the wedding, with her Paris home full of guests and laughter and the special tender radiance that seemed to surround the young couple, Sarah looked at Louis and wondered how much he knew.

Did he know what he had done for her? She had been so close to giving up until that day. Without the work she loved and the dignity of being an actress, she had been ready to die. She had *wanted* to die . . . and he had brought her back to life.

In the next few years she went on to play *Daniel* again on tour. In Madrid a huge crowd waited for her at the railroad station. When she was carried out of the train in her little chair, someone —moved to show honor in the only way he could think of—threw his coat on the ground in front of the two men who carried her chair. Others did the same. From the railway station to her waiting automobile hundreds of yards away, the ground was covered like a carpet with the coats of men who could say only in this way how much they loved her.

Then she did *La Gloire*, by Rostand, in Paris. After that Verneuil had another play ready for her. *Regine Armand*. It was about

187

the theater, and in it was one scene that always stopped the show while the audience burst into spontaneous applause. It was when one of the actors asked Regine Armand when she was going to rest and retire.

"Rest? Do I ever think of such a thing?" Sarah stormed at him. "Do you believe that I shall ever rest?"

It was so true to her own life that the audience always responded with this voluntary tribute.

Just the same, the time was coming. She was rehearsing a new play by Sascha Guitry which was to open the Christmas of 1922 when she was stricken with uremia. She recovered, fought her way back to a semblance of health and, when she found that her part in that play had been given to another actress, announced that she would do Corneille's *Rodogune*.

On March 14, before she could begin rehearsals, she was stricken again. On March 26, 1923, Sarah Bernhardt died.

Seldom had a funeral been seen like hers, in any city or nation of the world. Traffic in the whole of Paris was almost stopped for half the day.

From early in the morning the crowds waited, jamming the sidewalks and spilling through the police cordon into the streets. They waited until the coffin and the official procession had passed; then not even the police could stop them from joining in and walking behind. It was as if all of Paris moved in a solid body of people through the silent streets—thousands upon thousands of people.

Just behind the coffin, drawn by plumed horses, were automobiles piled with floral wreaths that had come from everywhere. Immediately behind them came the drummers.

It was the sound of the drums that brought a man from his desk to stand by the window and look down into the street. He was the same critic who had watched her performance in *Athalie*. He had been trying all morning to find the words to write her obituary for his newspaper, but they would not come. Now that throbbing sound called him to the window: that muffled, grave, solemn, majestic drumming that marks the passing of one who has worn France's Legion of Honor.

He saw behind the drummers the orderly lines of hundreds of famous people. Representatives of nations and their governments. World-renowned writers, actors, artists, statesmen.

Then he saw the people.

Offices had closed. Stores were shut. Schoolchildren were let out of school; housewives had left their tasks. The businessmen of Paris, the students of the Left Bank, the flower sellers and the women who had the stalls in the markets—all were there. They had been Sarah's audience when she was alive. Now they were her friends going with her a little way on her last journey.

A friend joined the critic at the window and together they watched the awesome spectacle below, slowly pacing in step to the drums.

"Someone said of Sarah Bernhardt," the friend remarked softly, "that her life 'was shot with thunder and lightning; it was a whirl-wind of dates, titles, gleaming swords, fireworks; poets and drama-tists, men of genius; smiles, prayers, and tears; applause, sobs; whistling trains, steamers; a babel of tongues, shouts of enthusiasm, cries of passion.'"

The critic nodded his head. "Well said. But the only tribute that can match what we are seeing today is what Francisque Sarcey wrote of her:

She is unique and no one will ever take her place.

189

INDEX

191